Identity and Modern Israeli Literature

Identity and Modern Israeli Literature

RISA DOMB
University of Cambridge

VALLENTINE MITCHELL
LONDON • PORTLAND, OR

First published in 2006 in Great Britain by
VALLENTINE MITCHELL
Suite 314, Premier House,
112–114 Station Road,
Edgware, Middlesex HA8 7BJ

and in the United States of America by
VALLENTINE MITCHELL
c/o ISBS, 920 NE 58th Avenue, Suite 300
Portland, OR 97213-3786

Website: www.vmbooks.com

Copyright © Risa Domb 2006

British Library Cataloguing in Publication Data
Domb, Risa
  Identity and modern Israeli literature
  1. Israeli fiction – History and criticism 2. Identity
  (Psychology) in fiction literature 3. Jews in literature 4. Jews –
  Identity
  I. Title
  892. 4'3609353

ISBN 0-85303-660-8 (paper)
ISBN 978-0-85303-660-9 (paper)

Library of Congress Cataloging-in-Publication Data
A catalog record has been applied for

All rights reserved. No part of this publication may be reproduced, stored in or introduced into a retrieval system or transmitted in any form or by any means, electronic, mechanical, photocopying, recording or otherwise, without the prior written permission of the publisher of this book.

Printed in Great Britain by Biddles Ltd, King's Lynn, Norfolk

For you Dicky,
With all my love,
Risa

Contents

	Acknowledgements	viii
1	Introduction	1
2	Language and Identity	11
3	'Ut Pictura Poesis': The Expression of Ideology in Nathan Shaham's *Series*	22
4	Touching the Pain: Memory and Identity in *The Last Jew* by Yoram Kaniuk	36
5	The Poetics of Unsaying: The Identity Crisis of the Modern Jew in *The Story of a Life* by Aharon Appelfeld	57
6	The Loneliness of the Wanderers: *Water Touching Water* by Sami Michael	67
7	Crossing Borders: The Clash of Civilizations in *The Liberating Bride* by A.B. Yehoshua	78
8	Nothing Is As It Was: Time and Change in *Heatwave and Crazy Birds* by Gabriela Avigur-Rotem	90
	Index	104

Acknowledgements

The author would like to thank the Faculty of Oriental Studies and Girton College for the grants awarded. Special thanks to Frances Gertler, my brilliant editor and friend.

Note
Book and story titles in the text and footnotes have been provided in Hebrew, English or both, where appropriate. Apparent oddities in the translations are consistent with the source, which often provides titles in both Hebrew and English, even where the book is available only in Hebrew.

1

Introduction

The study of imaginative literature is in many ways a profitable one for understanding the nation, in this case, the Israeli nation. The issues that are represented in literature, and which I would like to highlight in this book, exemplify the notion that 'the study of contemporary fiction ... is always a comment on the responsible practice of interpreting the images *today* – how to place them, how to give them perspective, how to discuss the way they reflect a submerged history while turning it into a contemporary, instantaneous shadow'.[1] The story of Israeli literature mirrors that of the State of Israel, and both are inextricably bound up with the story of Zionism.

The Zionist dream, conceived in the darker days of European Jewish history, was fulfilled with the move of Jews, albeit in relatively small numbers, from West to East: from a lengthy abnormal exilic existence in Europe, to a normal independent life in their ancestral homeland of Eretz Israel. In our own time, nationalism can be seen as the most significant new (or rather revived) ideology of Jewish identity, with the Hebrew language as its emblem. The Hebrew language, which was revived to become a spoken language, demonstrates a unique link between ideology, memory, Jewish identity and language.

Language, ideology, memory and cultural and national identity dominate Hebrew as well as Israeli literature. This book discusses each of them separately (synchronically rather than diachronically) and focuses mainly on prose writing, because it is the novel that historically accompanied the rise of nations. The rise of the modern nation-state in Europe in the late eighteenth and early nineteenth centuries is in many ways inseparable from the forms and subjects of imaginative literature.[2] The political task of nationalism directed the course of

Israeli literature into distinct national literature and, in turn, the literature participated in the formation of the nation.

All the works discussed here shed interesting light on aspects of language, ideology, memory and cultural and national identity, but each also has a central preoccupation that particularly illuminates one or more of these issues.

It seems appropriate to start by examining the impact of language, commonly perceived as the important component of any collective identity, on the development of the restructuring of Jewish identity. The association of linguistic distinctiveness with national culture became very strong in Europe during the nineteenth century, when the strong connection between cultural renaissance and political developments was acknowledged.[3] Also, the importance of language in the rise of European nationalism is relevant to the study of Israeli nationalism. In his study on nationalism, Benedict Anderson observes that:

> The old sacred languages – Latin, Greek and Hebrew – were forced to mingle on equal ontological footing with a motley plebeian vernacular rivals, in a movement which complemented their earlier demonition in the market-place by print-capitalism. If all languages now shared a common (intra-) mundane status, then all were in principle equally worthy of study and admiration. But by Who? Logically, since now none belonged to God, by their new owners: each language's native speakers – and readers. As Seton-West helpfully shows, the nineteenth-century was, in Europe and its immediate peripheries, a golden age of vernacularizing lexicographers, grammarians, philologists, and literatures. The energetic activities of these professional intellectuals were central to the shaping of nineteenth-century European nationalisms.[4]

To gain further perspective on the role of Hebrew in the development of Jewish nationalism, one could look at the important role of the language in the Russification of the heterogenous populations of the Tsars, particularly during the reign of Alexander III (1881–94), when Russian was made the compulsory language of instruction in all schools. It was there and then, and partly as a consequence, that Zionist ideology and the revival of the Hebrew language were being developed. The history of language is part of political, economic and social history, and particularly so in the case of the Hebrew language.

All the texts discussed in the following chapters have language as a central theme, but the treatment varies greatly from one to the other. Y.H. Brenner, Benjamin Tammuz and S.Y. Agnon tend to tackle it head-on, all writing at a time when the question of what language, and for whom, was at its most pressing. Nathan Shaham looks at how language both divides and brings people together. Aharon Appelfeld talks about the difficulties of finding any language in a post-Holocaust world to convey extreme experiences, and at what happens when an old language is dead or redundant and a new one alien, while Yoram Kaniuk explores the same territory but looks at how experience manifests itself into a language for living. His sense of language is more personal and intimate, looking at the disjunction between inner and outer dialogue, while A.B. Yehoshua is preoccupied with how different civilizations learn to coexist with others, and the role that language plays in bringing them together – or driving them apart. In *Heatwave and Crazy Birds*, Gabriela Avigur-Rotem uses sensuous prose and different styles of language to show the diverse origins of Israeli society and the disconnection between past and present. Sami Michael, whose first language was Arabic, has his protagonist share his own difficulty in adopting the Hebrew language and being to a great extent torn away from his natural mother tongue. All of these issues, which are present to a greater or lesser extent in the texts discussed – as indeed in many others by Hebrew and Israeli writers – show the centrality of language to identity.

Ideology is the second major issue dominating Hebrew/Israeli literature. Idealism and national aspirations in the context of unexpectedly harsh reality are the hallmarks of Hebrew literature of the period immediately preceding the establishment of the State of Israel. Zionist ideology, which defined Israeli identity, was unified and monolithic and accordingly up to 1967 only one voice was heard in literary texts: it was Ashkenazi (Jews of German or East European descent), male, socialist and politically identified with the left, and secular. After the realization of the basic Zionist dream – the foundation of the State of Israel – after the euphoria in the wake of independence, when Zionist ideology was institutionalized in statehood, the hitherto apparent cohesiveness of society began to be shaken, as the resolution of the one major issue cleared the way for other concerns to take centre-stage. Many cracks and divisions were soon apparent: secular versus religious; those who wanted to acknowledge the past versus those who wished to forget it; Ashkenazim versus Sephardim (Oriental Jews), and so on. In the wake of disillusionment, the literature of the 1960s and 1970s, the literature called 'The New Wave',[5] expressed alienation from society and shifted its vision from the collective to the individual. This deviated from the hitherto dominant ideology that insisted on the supremacy of the collective. And, as is often the case, changes in the development of Hebrew literature coincided with changes in Europe, which in turn were consequences of wider social and cultural transformations.

Modernism and Existentialism dominated European literature (for example, in the writings of Kafka, Camus, Beckett and Ionesco) and struck a chord with the younger generation of Israeli writers, who in turn began to portray marginal, displaced characters in their work. This led to a revival of the connection that had been severed between the Sabra generation of 1948 and European culture, and for the first time since its inception in the nineteenth century, Modern Hebrew literature turned back towards Western literature. This shift coincided with the political and economic circumstances that enabled Israeli writers to travel abroad more easily. The renewed encounter with Europe triggered admiration and attraction as well as hostility and repulsion. Some protagonists escape to Europe and others from Europe, but in both cases Europe never serves as just a tourist's sightseeing spot abroad but as a world which stands in total contrast to Israel, a theme overtly explored in Shaham's novel *Series* and Avigur-Rotem's *Heatwave and Crazy Birds*. It is much easier to ask fundamental questions about the nature of the whole Israeli enterprise when placing the fictional characters far away. Being away from the singular ideology which dominated their life in Israel, writers based their search on multiplicity of differences. Through their protagonists, many of them sought to define their ideology in terms of its relation to, or its difference from, other European ideologies. It was through the relation to the Other, the relation to what it was not, to what it lacked, that they were able to examine their own. Thus, the geographical distance served not so much the purpose of discovering the 'other', as of examining the self.[6]

Distance of time also facilitates the discovery of the self. The ability to re-inscribe the past, reactivate it, commits our understanding of the past, and our reinterpretation of the future.[7] Many contemporary writers began to explore the past, and depict the life of the early settlers, mainly in prose.[8] The ideological disorientation has inspired the search for readjusted definitions through fictionalized autobiographical retrospectives.[9] It seems that Israeli literature, particularly in the 1980s, sought to restore the lost paradise rather than find a new one. Utopia for them was the reality of the past, whereas the present is nothing but a great and ugly dystopia. But, as S. Yizhar suggested:

> perhaps there is no utopia in an open society, which succeeds in withstanding more than three generations: the founders' generation that undertook a mission, the generation of the sons, which internalised but also began to show some reservations, and the third generation, which no longer saw itself committed to the original dreams, and some of which even chose to draw away not only from the dreams but also from the place of the dreamers. Some explain the decline of utopia as a reaction to

all the wars in which Isaac was required to be sacrificed for Abraham's faith, war after war as historical landmarks branded as painful burns in every personal biography.[10]

In 1977 the Likud party, led by Menahem Begin, came to power, with the large Sephardi constituency coming into its own. This was a turning point. It signalled changes in Zionist ideology, and greater pluralism. Writers of 'Oriental', or 'Sephardi', origin began to express pride in their roots and reflect their societies before their immigration to Israel. Several authors focus on the Oriental Jewish community in their different countries of origin.[11] In his novel *A Journey to the End of the Millennium*,[12] A.B. Yehoshua explores the different cultural codes of Ashkenazi and Sephardi communities, reminding us of their interaction in the distant past, towards the end of the first millennium. He points out that Jewish culture was, and should be, regarded as a pluralistic culture.[13] Ethnic diversity and diversity of geographical origins have become increasingly recognized and appreciated in Israel. This is in line with a resurgent concern with ethnicity across Europe as a whole.[14] (Incidentally, the change in the mainstream Israeli experience meant greater openness in literature, and a pluralism of voices emerged, including those of women writers.)[15] Another new trend in the 1990s was for books whose centre is not the Zionist narrative, but the Jewish community in Europe before and after the Second World War.[16] Yet, with all the changes and the multitude of voices heard amongst the generation of the 1980s and 1990s, the object of their confrontation is still more often than not the Zionist text. It remained the one spiritual presence, whose contents and messages, even when deflated, were loaded with new meanings according to what in the Israeli experience was most relevant to the writers.[17] Thus, the main themes in many contemporary writings are Zionist and Sabra ideologies. Questioning and examining the two lead to another theme, which is the search for the self, particularly vis-à-vis Jewish identity.

In discussing questions of cultural identity, Stuart Hall suggested that,

> Identities are about questions of using the resources of history, language and culture in the process of becoming rather than of being ... Identities are therefore constituted within, not outside representation ... Precisely because identities are constructed within, not outside discourse, we need to understand them as produced in specific historical and institutional sites within specific discursive formations and practices, by specific enunciative strategies.[18]

This general definition of identity is highly relevant to Israeli identity, particularly since in recent years many Israelis have been deeply involved in examining and analysing their national identity. Also speaking generally, Terry Eagleton defined culture as the 'complex of values, customs, beliefs and practices which constitute the way of life of a specific group ... It now means the affirmation of a specific identity.'[19] It has been suggested that, 'the further the secular Israeli Jew goes away from the original Zionist models, so does the literature increase its contemplation and investigations concerning the problem of identity'.[20] Be that as it may, the concept of identity shifted from the concept of the myth of the New Jew in the early settlement,[21] to the undermining of the myth of the Sabra in the post-modern and post-Zionist literature of the late 1980s and early 1990s.[22] Israeli identity, which was shaped by the founders of Israeli nationalism, the early Zionists of the late nineteenth and early twentieth centuries, has changed. In the 1920s the model of the 'New Jew' was transformed to become the 'New Hebrew'. In the late 1930s and in the 1940s, it became the native 'Sabra'.[23] The 1950s witnessed the dominance of the 'Israeli',[24] which during the 1960s and 1970s, became Jewish/Israeli.[25] A.B. Yehoshua regards this 'neo-Judaism' as a process of reconciliation between early Zionism and Judaism.[26] The effects of the Holocaust on all aspects of Israeli life, increased ethnic awareness and the new phenomenon of the 'born again' Jew, brought about a Judaisation of the secular society. Having identified themselves as Israelis, the writers and their protagonists have become Israeli Jews.

All the writers discussed in this book are preoccupied with the nature of what it means to be Israeli. In particular, the complexity of defining Israeli identity is highlighted by Shaham in his novel, *Series*, in which his protagonists struggle to find representative characters for the film they are making (see p.23). Kaniuk, too, in *The Last Jew*, explores the overlaying of identities that occurs over time, the necessary and essential merging of the Jewish and Israeli experience, while Appelfeld looks at the identity crisis of the modern Jew and, like Kaniuk, also looks for a reconciliation between early Zionism and Judaism. Despite the differences in their approach, all seem in one way or another to be advocating an integration of the Jewish experience into contemporary Israeli living.

Amos Almog observed that the Israeli Sabra, who became more and more secular, disappeared from the arena of Israeli history, together with the Zionist religion which had created him. He forecasts that a new 'Israeli religion' will emerge.[27] Interestingly, he, like many others, speaks about national identity in terms of 'religion'. In one of the articles in a recently published book entitled *We, the Secular Jews*, and subtitled *What is Jewish Secular Religion?*, Yair Tsaban explains this uniquely Jewish phenomenon.[28] There seems to be a complete overlap between religious identity and national identity in Judaism. For religious Jews this is an important principle of their faith. However, Jewish Emancipation together with modern nationalism came about as a result of the process of secularization in Europe. Only in this context can one explain the emergence of Zionism when it did. According to the Zionist Tsaban, this meant victory over the domination of the Jewish religion, and finding a non-religious expression to Jewish history, Jewish culture and the love for Eretz Israel. This new challenge was the main reason for the objection of the orthodox community to Zionism. They not only feared it to be 'false messianism', but they were afraid that Zionism would provide the Jews with a new option of Jewish identity, an alternative option to that which religious Judaism had provided for generations. Indeed, Zionism did offer a new Jewish national identity, independent of religious identity. A.B. Yehoshua endorses this sentiment by declaring that if he were asked to describe himself on his identity card as a secular Jew, he would reply: 'First of all, I do not use the term "secular Jew", but I use the term "Israeli". Full stop.'[29] However, the notion of having a new Jewish identity independent of a religious identity obviously includes the Arab population, regardless of religious affiliation. Yosef Oren warns that if Israeli identity becomes a civil identity, the Jews in Israel will lose their common identity with Jews outside Israel.[30] In a much later interview with Yotam Reuveny, A.B. Yehoshua suggested that the rise of anti-Semitism in the twenty-first century is due to the inseparable connection between religion and nationality which is inherent in Jewish identity:[31]

> the sense of lack of any borders to Jewish identity, which can penetrate to any place, to be seen just like the gentile, in dress, in language and in customs and so on, but still can contain within itself an unidentifiable kernel of identity just like the Marrano in Spain, who despite the fact that they changed their religion could still maintain their Jewish identity. For the identity is in the consciousness and not in some external object. This is the essential thing about our identity, its lack of boundaries, which Zionism was attempting to correct.[32]

The gap between the religious option and the non-religious option has become wide in Israel today. Yet, surprisingly, this problem is so far hardly reflected in fictional works. There is only an increasing number of works in which the religious life is reflected from within. Perhaps this phenomenon deserves a separate study. Amos Oz, in one of his essays, suggests that the gaps have existed in Judaism throughout the long history of preceding generations.[33] Therefore, the gap between those who adhere to 'Halachic Judaism', and those who do not live by the *Shulchan Aruch* (the code of Jewish law written by Joseph Caro and first printed in 1565) is not quite as alarming as the media would lead us to believe. The gap could be bridged, according to Oz, if we could separate Jewish religion from the exclusive possession of the religious. Zionist ideology and Israeli identity are in a state of disorientation. Yet, disorientation, so typical to modernity, is a result of openness and pluralization of social life, as well as an increase of choices.[34] Amid a puzzling diversity of options and possibilities, one of the more attractive choices for Israelis suggested by A.B. Yehoshua, is the reconciliation between early Zionism and Judaism.[35] Secular Israelis today re-open their old 'Jewish Bookcase', to draw from it new meanings which are relevant to them. However, the situation has become alarming since the gap between orthodox and secular segments of Israeli society assumed political dimensions. This is perhaps not surprising. Zionist ideology sought to re-define Jewish identity, and thereby linked ideology and identity to become inseparable from one another.[36] The Frankfurt School Marxist Theodor Adorno (1903–69), argued against ideology and the principle of identity, because both 'homogenize' the world, equating distinct phenomena, and suppressing all contradiction. According to him ideology is a 'totalitarian' system which has managed and processed all social conflict out of existence, and identity is the 'primal form' of all ideology.[37] Only art speaks up for the differential and non-identical, promoting the claims of the sensuous particular against the tyranny of some seamless totality. One could argue against Adorno's critique, as Terry Eagleton does, by pointing out that the real ideological conditions of Western societies are far from being totalitarian, and are mixed and self-contradictory.[38] However, what is relevant here is that the two opposing sides of this argument acknowledge that identity and ideology are closely interlinked, as indeed is the case with Zionism. Nathan Shaham's novel *Series*[39] is one of many novels which represent the complex link between ideology and identity, and demonstrates that the conflict between the two is inescapable.[40]

Memory is undoubtedly an integral part of cultural and national identity, and this is particularly the case with Jewish nationalism, or Zionism. Anthony Smith argues against modernist scholars of nationalism, such as Eric Hobsbawm, Ernest Gellner and Ellie Kedourie, who he believes fail to accord weight to the pre-existing cultures and ethnic ties of the nations that emerged in the modern epoch. Thus, his historical ethno-symbolism emerges from the theoretical critique of these modernist approaches. Smith proposes that for ethno-symbolists, 'what gives nationalism its power are the myths, memories, traditions, and symbols of ethnic heritages and the ways in which a popular *living past* has been, and can be, rediscovered and reinterpreted by modern nationalist intelligentsias. It is from these elements of myth, memory, symbol, and tradition that modern national identities are reconstituted in each generation.'[41] He regards nations as historical phenomena because they embody shared memories, traditions and hopes. Zionism was created on the basis of the experiences of earlier generations and of shared memories of Jewish history associated with a specific territory which they regarded as their homeland. 'On this basis arises a shared culture, often a common language or customs or religion, the product of the common historical experiences that give rise to shared memories.'[42] This is a theme that preoccupies all of the writers discussed here, whether they are looking for a language in which to express the memory of the inexpressible (Appelfeld); discussing the importance of integrating memories of the past in order to move on to a psychologically healthy future (Shaham and Avigur-Rotem); or trying to find a balance between appropriate personal and collective memory and the kind of memories that paralyse or poison individuals and societies (Kaniuk). The writers are looking not only at the memory of the Holocaust and other conflicts, but also at the shared memory of the Jews, their common experience and their differences – different languages, culture, places of origin – and at whether and how a successful nation can ever integrate its collective past in such a way as to enable it to move on to a healthy, fulfilled future.

NOTES

1. Timothy Brennan, 'The National Longing for Form', in Homi K. Bhabha (ed), *Nation and Narration* (London and New York: Routledge, 1990), p.67.
2. Ibid., p.48.
3. See David McCrone, 'Inventing the Past: History and Nationalism', in idem, *The Sociology of Nationalism: Tomorrow's Ancestors* (London and New York: Routledge, 1998), pp.44–63.
4. Benedict Anderson, *Imagined Communities* (London: Verso, 1991), pp.70–1.
5. This term was coined by Gershon Shaked.
6. For an extended analysis of the subject, see R. Domb, *Home Thoughts From Abroad* (London and Portland, OR: Vallentine Mitchell, 1996).
7. For more on this subject see Homi Bhabha, 'Cultures In-Between', in Stuart Hall and Paul du Gay (eds), *Questions of Cultural Identity* (London, California, India: Sage Publications, 1996), p.59.
8. It is interesting to note that a similar exploration of the past is evident in Israeli cinema, particularly that of the Sabra generation of the 1948 War of Independence. See Miri Talmon, *Israeli Graffiti: Nostalgia, Groups, and Collective Identity in Israeli Cinema* (Tel Aviv: Open University of Israel, 2001).
9. For example, H. Bartov, D. Shahar, Y. Ben-Ner, N. Alloni, B. Tammuz, Y. Kenaz.
10. From a lecture entitled 'Utopia and Poetry', delivered in Cambridge, UK, March 1998.

11. D. Benayah Serry, A. Swissa, S. Michael, E. Amir, R. Matalon.
12. A.B. Yehoshua, *A Journey to the End of the Millennium* (Tel Aviv: Hakibbutz Hameuchad, 1997).
13. For more on this see Nissim Calderon, *Multiculturalism Versus Pluralism in Israel* (Tel Aviv: Haifa University Press & Zmora Bitan, 1998), pp.19–36.
14. For more on the subject see Kevin Robins, 'Interrupting Identities: Turkey/Europe', in Hall and du Gay (eds), *Questions of Cultural Identity*, p.75.
15. H. Bat-Shahar, O. Castel-Bloom, Y. Katzir and S. Liebrecht are from the new generation of women novelists that has emerged in the last decade. B. Gur introduced the popular detective novel, making a conscious break from the seriousness which has dominated Modern Hebrew literature since its inception.
16. Y. Hoffman, Y. Birstein, G. Avigur-Rotem, and others.
17. Y. Berlovitz, *Lehamtzi Eretz, Lehamtzi Am* [Inventing a Land, Inventing a People] (Tel Aviv: Hakibbutz Hameuchad, [n.d.]), pp.244–55.
18. Hall and du Gay (eds), *Questions of Cultural Identity*, p.4.
19. Terry Eagleton, *The Idea of Culture* (Oxford: Blackwell, 2000), pp.34–8.
20. See, for example, David Ohana's *The Last Israelis* (Tel Aviv: Hakibbutz Hameuchad, 1998), in which he argues with the New Historians. He seeks to replace the model of the New Jew with that of a Mediterranean Jew.
21. As, for example, in B. Tammuz, *Requiem for Na'aman* (Tel Aviv: Zmora Bitan, 1978); and *Ya'acov* (Sifriyat Makor, 1971); Y. Kaniuk, *The Last Jew* (Tel Aviv: Hakibbutz Hameuchad, Sifriyat Poalim 1982); A. Megged, *Al Etzim Va'avanim* [Of Trees and Stones] (Tel Aviv: Am Oved, 1974 [1973]); and Dan Tsalka, *Philip Arbes* (Tel Aviv: Zmora Bitan, 1996 [1977]).
22. As in O. Castel-Bloom, *Dolly City* (Tel Aviv: Zmora Bitan, 1992). In Meir Shalev's novel *Roman Russi* [A Russian Novel] (Tel Aviv: Am Oved, 1989), the Zionist project of the pioneering fathers is turned into a place of burial for Jews from the Diaspora.
23. As is represented, for example, in S. Yizhar's *Mikdamot* (Tel Aviv: Zmora Bitan, 1992); and idem, *Tsalhabim* (Tel Aviv: Zmora Bitan, 1993).
24. As is represented, for example, in A. Megged, *Ha-hai al hamet* [The Living and the Dead] (Tel Aviv: Am Oved, 1968).
25. As represented, for example, in B. Tammuz's trilogy *Elyakum* (Jerusalem: Keter, 1988); and in N. Shaham's *Series* (Tel Aviv: Am Oved, 1992).
26. A.B. Yehoshua, *Hakir ve-hahar* [The Wall and the Mountain] (Tel Aviv: Zmora Bitan, 1989), p.56.
27. A. Almog, 'Amud Esh Hadash' [New Column of Fire], *Poetica*, 42–3 (Jan. 1992), p.13.
28. Dadi Zuker (ed.), *Anoo Ha-Yehoodim Ha-Hilonim, Mahi Zehoot Hilonit?* (Yediot Ahronot, 1999), pp.111–31.
29. Yehoshua, *Hakir ve-hahar*, p.210.
30. Yosef Oren, *The Writing as Political Announcement* (Rishon Letsion: Yahad, 1992), pp.90–1.
31. Yotam Reuveny, *Diokan 2, Abraham B. Yehoshua: Two interviews and notes* (Tel Aviv: Nimrod, 2003).
32. Ibid., p.44.
33. Amos Oz, *Kol Ha-tikvot, Mahshavot 'al Zehut* [Thoughts on Identity] (Jerusalem: Keter, 1998), p.50.
34. For further discussion on the subject see A. Giddens, *Modernity and Self-Identity* (London: Polity Press, 1991), pp.1–9.
35. Yehoshua, *Hakir ve-hahar*, p.56.
36. See, for example, the study by Oz Almog, *Hatsabar-Dyokan* [The Sabra: A Profile] (Tel Aviv: Am Oved, 1997).
37. Terry Eagleton, *Ideology* (London: Verso, 1991), p.126; Theodor Adorno, *Aesthetic Theory* (London: Continuum, 1984).
38. Eagleton, *Ideology*, p.128.
39. Nathan Shaham, *Series* (Tel Aviv: Am Oved, 1992).
40. Irving Howe, *Politics and the Novel* (New York: New American Library, 1987), p.20.
41. Anthony D. Smith, *Myth and Memories of the Nation* (Oxford: Oxford University Press, 1999), p.9.
42. Ibid., p.208.

2

Language and Identity

The development of the Hebrew language demonstrates a unique link between language and identity, which may explain why Hebrew has never died. Although in our own times, nationalism can be seen as the most significant new (or revived) factor of Jewish identity, there is no doubt that the Hebrew language is its most distinctive emblem.

This link between language and national identity was expressed during the visit of the President of the State of Israel, Ezer Weitzman, to the German Bundestaag on 16 January 1996, when he declared:

> We have created a unique cultural miracle, we have resuscitated our language, our Hebrew language ... We and our language are alive. We, who have risen from the ashes, and the language – which has been waiting in shrouds of Torah scrolls and in pages of prayer books – are both alive. The language that was whispered only in synagogues, which was sung only in religious rituals, which was screamed in the gas chambers – in the 'Shema Yisroel' prayer – has been resuscitated ... These two dead things that have been revived after so many years – the Jewish State and the Hebrew language – are the very essence of our existence in this century.[1]

The intimate link between the Hebrew language and the identity of the Jewish people is explored again and again in Modern Hebrew literature. The arguments often assume ideological, as well as linguistic, dimensions. The texts discussed in this chapter explore the manifestations of this debate and shed an interesting light on the relationship between literature and ideology in general. In each text a different ideology is crystallized through a discussion about the Hebrew language. By focusing on one specific theme and setting aside other considerations of the texts and their aesthetic value, it is possible to see their subservience to ideology.

The debate stretches as far back as the nineteenth century. In his earlier writings, one of the leading poets of early Modern Hebrew literature Y.L. Gordon (1830–92) expressed the belief that the study of Hebrew was the key to continuing Jewish cultural advancement and ultimately to the attainment of European Enlightenment. In doing this, he was articulating one of the major aims of the Jewish Enlightenment movement, the Haskalah, which was to propagate the revival of the ancient language in its written secular form as one of the main tools for the redefinition of Jewish identity. However, towards the end of his life, Gordon drew attention to the difficulty he and other Haskalah writers had in continuing to write literature in Hebrew, which led either to extreme orthodoxy or to writers turning their backs on the language and thereby gradually becoming assimilated.

In a poem entitled 'For Whom Do I Toil', first published in the journal *Ha-Shahar* in 1870–1, Gordon writes of his disappointment in the younger generation of European Jews who did not heed Haskalah ideology and who abandoned Hebrew altogether:

> And our sons? The generation to come?
> From childhood they take leave of us,
> For them above all my heart bleeds.
> They go forward year after year,
> Who knows how wide?
> Perhaps whither there is no return.
> For whom, then, do I toil, I mere mortal,
> For the handful remaining lovers of Hebrew
> Who have not yet mocked her or scorned?...
> Yes, to you I sacrifice my soul and my tears
> I weep on your shoulders and share my pain
> I grasp you and embrace you again and again
> O who can foresee the future, who can say
> Am I the last of Zion's poets and you, the last readers?[2]

This poem illustrates that though the two were by no means synonymous, the Haskalah movement enlisted Hebrew literature to help promote its ideas.[3] This overt subservience to ideology might account for its poetic faults.

Disillusioned with the results of Haskalah ideology and with Haskalah literature, the next generation of Hebrew writers, the writers of the Age of Revival (1880–1920), sought to shift the emphasis from the collective to the individual: the Haskalah writer was always the social thinker and preacher, and made no distinction between fictional literature and publicist writing; all were there to serve the same ends. The new Revivalist writers examined the literary achievements of their predecessors, rejecting their literary norms and criticizing their limited ideological strategies.[4] Yet their belief in Hebrew as the only suitable national language remained constant. The only debate was over the role of Hebrew in the attainment of ideological goals and whether Hebrew should be used as a vehicle to promote Zionism. Even though doubts were expressed by writers such as Ahad Ha-Am, whose 'For whom do We Write in Hebrew' is a clear echo of Gordon's 'For Whom Do I Toil?', nevertheless he and other writers such as M.Y. Berdichevsky, H.M. Bialik and S. Tchernichovsky, were among many who continued to write in Hebrew.

It has been suggested that in addition to the limiting didactic element inherent in Haskalah literature, one of the main reasons for its artistic failure was its denial of its Yiddish influence in favour of 'pure' biblical Hebrew.[5] However, the Hebrew used in different parts of the world always manifests the influence of the surrounding vernacular. Rabbinic Hebrew can be seen as Hebrew in Aramaic syntax, with a great number of words borrowed from Greek and Roman. The language of the Tibbonites, the great translators of the writings of medieval Jewish philosophers from Arabic into Hebrew, is very much influenced by Arabic. The Hebrew written in Eastern Europe from the medieval period to the sixteenth and seventeenth centuries was greatly influenced by spoken Yiddish. However, unlike these examples, Haskalah literature resisted external linguistic influences. Yet, despite its limited artistic achievements, the contribution of the revival of the written Hebrew of the Haskalah to the revival of spoken Hebrew should not be underestimated.

Mendele Mocher Sfarim (1835–1917) the creator of a new Hebrew style, the *noosach*, departed from the 'purity' of the language advocated during the early Haskalah period, instead blending biblical and post-biblical Hebrew for the first time in the history of Hebrew literature. He employed the syntax of classical Hebrew, and in addition, integrated elements of spoken Yiddish.[6] The writers of the Age of Revival (such as Ahad Ha-Am, Berdichevsky and U.N. Gnessin) chose to adopt German and Russian syntax as well, and all these influences serve as a basis for spoken Hebrew today.

Eliezer Ben-Yehuda (1858–1922), one of the so-called Fathers of the revival of spoken Hebrew, had an enormous impact on the development of Modern Hebrew language and literature. Although responsible for a monumental Hebrew dictionary, he is regarded by some first and foremost as a man of politics rather than a professional linguist.[7] Ben-Yehuda was a key figure during the struggle of Hebrew to establish itself as the official teaching language in schools in Israel at the turn of the century. As early as 1879, in his first published essay 'An Important Question', he stressed the link between the Hebrew language and Jewish nationalism. This theme was to recur in his memoirs *A Dream Come True* (1917–18)[8] in which he proposed that 'the ingathering of the exiles from all over the world, emanating from Zionist ideology, could succeed only in Hebrew.' Significantly, the first word that he coined in Hebrew (because there was no biblical precedent for it) was *'le'umoot'* (subsequently to become *le'umioot*) 'nationalism'. Even today, the difficulties of the old ancient Hebrew in coping with contemporary concepts is still complex, as expressed by Yehuda Amichai in his poem 'National Thoughts':

> Caught in a homeland-trap:
> To talk now in this tired tongue,
> Torn out of its sleep in the Bible: blinded,
> It totters from mouth to mouth. In a tongue that described
> Miracles and God, now to say: automobile, bomb, God.
>
> The square letters wanted to remain
> Closed: every letter a locked house,
> To remain and to be enclosed in a final D
> And sleep in it forever.[9]

This dichotomy notwithstanding, the debate about the role of the language in the revival of national ideology became a theme explored in, and exemplified by, many literary texts.[10] Answering questions such as how, and to what extent, Hebrew literature should be bound to ideological dictates dominated many literary works. Writers shifted their interests from the promotion of European Enlightenment to the reassessment of Jewish self-definition and to the propagation of Zionist nationalism.

This shift in focus is central to Y.H. Brenner's second autobiographical novel, *Around the Point* (1904),[11] set in a small town in the Pale of Settlement on the eve of the 1905 Russian Revolution. The life of Ya'akov Abramson, the protagonist, is intertwined with that of the collective. He epitomizes the young intellectual, 'uprooted' Jew of his generation (the *Talush*), who rejects the world of the old Jewish tradition of his father, yet is unable to gain a foothold in European culture, and is forever searching for self-definition. Abramson's search pivots around three 'points': Zionism, Socialism and the private destiny of the Individual. Just like M.Z. Feierberg's protagonist in the late nineteenth-century novella *Whither* before him, Abramson is unable to separate himself from the collective, and instead oscillates between the only two remaining 'points' or options before him.[12] Disillusioned by Socialism, as a last resort he turns to Zionism and becomes a Hebrew writer.

These two diametrically opposed political forces, Zionism and Socialism, preoccupy the protagonists of much of Brenner's work. Abramson epitomizes Jewish Zionism, while his Jewish girlfriend Hava Blumin, epitomizes mainstream Russian Socialism. Tragically, the gulf between these two forces cannot be bridged, and the relationship is doomed to failure. Having published an article on the influence of eighteenth-century Hasidism on the revived Hebrew literature of the nineteenth century, Abramson is engaged in writing a major article on Hebrew literature of the early part of the twentieth century. Much to Hava Blumin's surprise and disappointment, Abramson writes in Hebrew. She argues that he is wasting his time and efforts, as he has no reading public, and can reach but a few Hebrew readers, to which he responds: 'I am Hebrew, and I write Hebrew for the Hebrews!' He is concerned only with his people, in whose language he must speak. This argument is clearly self-referential, reflecting Brenner's own dilemma and conclusion.

In moments of elation Abramson is thrilled to be a Hebrew writer just at the time when 'Judaism liberated itself and is filled with new content'. Every now and again, however, he is tormented by doubts about the futility of writing in Hebrew. He becomes disheartened and feels that the Hebrew language is like the lone sheaf of corn over a great deep grave. What upsets him most is that he is writing in a language foreign to Hava Blumin. In a desperate attempt to get closer to her he decides to write an article in Russian whose subject is, not surprisingly, nationalism, but his weak nerves give way, he burns all his writing, and finally goes mad.

Brenner uses fiction to endorse Berdichevsky's earlier promotion of the ideology of the Age of Revival, and advocate the use of the Hebrew language as a viable literary medium. Despite Abramson's impotence on the collective and personal level, the only way forward is to resist universal ideologies, whether liberalism or socialism, and to continue to strive for a national solution. But Abramson fails, perhaps because, essentially, Hebrew needed to be united with its people for both to thrive.

The polarization between the universal and the national, the public and the individual, are central to Benjamin Tammuz's much later story, 'The Troops of the Defenders of the Hebrew Language' (1979),[13] which takes the debate a step further, and in new circumstances. Because the story was written at this much later date, though set pre-

Statehood, the battle could now be viewed from the other side, from the historical perspective in which Hebrew had prevailed and the European influence had been eschewed.

In Tammuz's story, the characters have taken up the Zionist option and left Europe for mandatory Palestine. Written Hebrew has won the day and now the fight is for spoken Hebrew. The doubts of Brenner's characters have receded, and the stance for the implementation of the Hebrew language is ruthless. However, Chorny, the protagonist, is a Russian poet lost when trying to translate his work into Hebrew. Having managed to translate it first into prose, however, with the help of a friend, Victor, he succeeds in turning this into Hebrew verse. Victor is also an immigrant, from Constantinople, who has abandoned his own mother tongue and adopted Hebrew, believing that the revival of the language is the only way to unite all Jews in Palestine. To his consternation, Chorny is rooted in Russian culture. The Russian spoken by his newly-arrived communist friend is like music to Chorny's ears, even though he knows he should abandon Russian. He confesses to Victor: 'In my head I am with you and I am with Hebrew. But, the heart is a physiological matter.' Victor's response is to join The Troops of the Defenders of the Language.

With irony and humour, the narrator describes the earnest attack at night on a window of a shop selling household and office goods (in mandatory Tel Aviv), because it was called 'Rivoli'. Members of the Troops compose a letter attached to a stone and thrown through the window: 'Hebrew, Speak Hebrew! The Hebrew Yishuv will not tolerate foreign names in its streets! If you wish to avoid worse damage in the future, choose a Hebrew name for your business. And here are some suggestions: "charm of the home", "glory of the dwelling", "beauty of the flat", "comfort". Signed: Anonymous zealots for the Hebrew language.' These ridiculous suggestions reveal the tone of the speaker, for it was impossible to totally obliterate European influence on the New Hebrew society, and highlights the fact that there were no suitable names available that weren't drawn from Europe, since the concepts themselves were foreign to Israel and to Hebrew. Victor represents the Zionist ideology which leaves no room for doubts, no room for deviation. The needs of the collective have to come before the needs of the individual. The authorial voice espouses this view but also makes us see how cruel and inflexible it is, what a high price the individual, in this case Victor, is asked to pay in having his language, in effect, shut down. Behind it all looms Tammuz's heretical question: was it really worth it? Was the decision of the arrogant Sabras, the indigenous Israelis, to turn their back on European culture and erase their cultural, linguistic identity, and choose a new direction worthwhile? Was it desirable? Or was it all an illusion?[14] (The question of what has been accomplished is also tackled head-on by Avigur-Rotem in *Heatwave and Crazy Birds*, see p.91.)

This revisionist view of the Zionist dream and the continuing debate so many years on of the value of his personal sacrifices, would have devastated Brenner's Abramson. In Tammuz's story, the drive to use the Hebrew language is identified with the pursuit of the national Zionist dream. At the same time it raises some questions about the direction it has taken. This direction, which led to the dissociation of the Sabra generation from European as well as from Jewish culture, was subsequently revised in favour of re-embracing Jewish roots. The Post-Modernist era has come full circle and turned towards Western literature for its inspiration, with novels whose titles, for example, *Dolly City* (by Orly Castel-Bloom) and *My First Sony* (by Benny Barabash), were English, written using Hebrew characters.

An altogether different ideology, albeit connected to the issue of identity, is presented in one of the stories of Israel's first ever Nobel prize winner, S.Y. Agnon. Agnon's story of 1950 *Ido VeEnam* (*Ido and Enam*) is usually considered his most enigmatic and complicated.[15] One of its less obvious aspects is the theme of Hebrew and its use as an ideological strategy in the narration. The meaning of the obscure title emerges only in the course of the story, and is the name of two supposedly lost languages. The narrator, who is looking after his friends' house in Jerusalem during their absence, is excited to discover that their tenant is none other than the 'world famous' scholar, Ginath.[16] We learn that:

> Even with his first published article, 'Ninety-nine Words of the Edo Language', Ginath had drawn the attention of many philologists; when he followed this up with his 'Grammar of Edo', no philologist could afford to ignore him. But what made him famous was his discovery of the Enamite Hymns. To discover ninety-nine words of a language whose very name was hitherto unknown was no small achievement, and a greater one still was the compilation of a grammar for this forgotten tongue. But the Enamite Hymns were more: they were not only a new-found link in the chain that bound the beginnings of recorded history to the ages before, but in themselves were splendid and incisive works. Not for nothing, then, did the greatest of scholars come to grips with them, and those who at first doubted that they were authentic Enamite texts began to compose commentaries on them.[17]

On the surface of the text there seems to be an overt admiration for the study and discovery of obscure languages, but when juxtaposed with an explanation of what this 'language' actually was, Agnon's brilliant irony is revealed.[18] While travelling to distant forgotten lands in pursuit of manuscripts, just as his counterpart Ginath has done, another character, Gamzu,[19] who collects ancient Jewish manuscripts, comes across a Jewish tribe whose speech he has difficulty in understanding, as their 'Hebrew has more full vowels and fewer elided syllables than ours and they pronounce words differently'. It transpires that this strange language is in fact made up: Gamzu's host and his host's daughter Gemula, who becomes his wife and follows him to Israel, invented it and therefore no one other than themselves can understand it. Hearing the songs and not knowing their origins, the scholar Ginath eagerly transcribes some of them, and ironically it is these that win him international acclaim.

Agnon criticizes the futile activities of scholars such as Ginath, who rather than studying their own culture, turn to obscure and forgotten cultures elsewhere.[20] Gamzu has also studied hymns, prayers and poetry, but does not make a name for himself because his Jewish sources are regarded as mere folklore. Another negative view of Hebrew and Jewish sources is held by the supposedly highly-cultured Greifenbach (the narrator's friend) and his wife:

> Greifenbach was not looking for books in Hebrew, even less for manuscripts and first editions. The little Hebrew he knew had been learned with difficulty. Although he prided himself on his sound knowledge of the language and its grammar, all this amounted to was biblical grammar he had studied in Gesenius' textbook on the structure of Hebrew. His wife managed better than he, for although her grammar was an amateur affair and she knew nothing of Gesenius, she could go on in Hebrew with her cleaning woman Grazia, and with the street traders too. All the same, Hebrew books were none of her concern.[21]

It has been pointed out that in order to explain Jewish history, Agnon presents two alternative concepts in this story: traditional Jewish orientation on the one hand, represented by Gamzu, and Canaanite, mythologically oriented on the other, represented by Ginath.[22] The story was published during the height of the controversy surrounding the Canaanite movement. The Canaanite movement, formed in the mid-1940s, called on the Jews in Eretz Israel to cut their links with the post-exilic Jewish past and to draw instead on the pre-rabbinic phase. The movement regarded the vast area of the 'Fertile Crescent' as having a common culture and hence as being one nation. This geo-historical philosophy, which advocated the natural territory absorbing into itself any ethnic group and digesting them into one nation of culture, was the foundation of the Canaanite doctrine. The Canaanites believed that there existed a mutual link between certain 'geography' and the 'history' that occurred within it. Ginath represents this belief and his interest lies in collecting only the hymns, prayers and poetry of the heroic and pre-exilic era, whereas Gamzu collects those of the Jewish era. One of the central questions posed in the story is whether Israeli culture should draw for its cultural identity on Ugaritic and pre-Jewish Near Eastern sources, or whether it should draw on historical Halachic Judaism. Agnon's stand is clear. The academic, geo-historical alternative which Ginath offers, despite its aesthetic and secular attraction, cannot and should not compete with Jewish prayers and hymns.[23] It is the Canaanite's mythological vision for which Ginath longs, and against which Agnon is warning: only the study of Hebrew and traditional Hebrew sources should be the basis of a Jewish identity.[24]

A final and interesting example of how the discussion about Hebrew can at once embody and also be used to express an ideology, is a poem by Yona Wallach. This introduces a new dimension, feminism, into the discussion of what language, specifically Hebrew, can convey. In her long poem entitled 'Hebrew',[25] Wallach stresses that the determination of gender in language is based upon arbitrary distinctions. Ironically, the inherent tension of language, Hebrew in particular, inevitably enacts the very thing that it seeks to objectify and correct or change. She deconstructs the feminine/masculine opposition, and illustrates how all forms of language are sites of struggle between these oppositions. She plays on the linguistic phenomenon where, in Hebrew there is only one word to denote 'sex' or 'gender' (*'min'*) by interchanging these two concepts:

> In English gender enjoys all the possibilities...
>
> Every I is genderless...
>
> Hebrew discriminates in favour or against...
>
> Hebrew is sex-obsessed
> Wants to know who is speaking...
>
> The language observes you naked
> My father did not allow me to look
> He turned his back when he peed
> I never saw him really clearly
> He always hid his sex...
>
> We can pass over sex
> We can give it up
> Who can tell the sex of a chick?...

Signs of male and female in a sentence
Give strange gender relations...

In his analysis of the poem, Arnold Band suggests that 'Wallach seems to counter that gender differences in language are only linguistic signs ... She would rather regard this linguistic gender differentiation as the potential play of the forces of nature as represented in the language.'[26] Surely this conclusion does not suggest that 'the "feminist" argument ... seems to be rejected by the poetess', but on the contrary, gives the argument an added dimension. Wallach is striving to make gender independent of sexuality and to move beyond the polarization of gender. She attacks the traditional male and female binary approach of discourse on gender. This binary approach gives license to discriminatory conceptions of the sexes and allows discourse itself to become gendered.[27]

Thus while each of the texts discussed here represents or proposes a different ideology, in all of them the debate is crystallized in a discussion about the Hebrew language, and in every one, the choice of language is intrinsic to a search for identity, whether national, religious, cultural or gender oriented.

The question of the use of the Hebrew language thus extends beyond the specific debate over the language itself and assumes a wider, metaphorical dimension. It has become an all-encompassing debate about the identity of the Jewish people: their roots, their religion and the way forward, not only in language but in every aspect of their being; their language is inseparable from their identity.

NOTES

1. Some historians today examine the negative cultural effects of a language being subverted by ideological motivations. Eli Shai, for example, suggests that the price of linking Modern Hebrew and the Zionist Movement and the State was very high and caused 'linguistic and intellectual brain-washing', *Ma'ariv*, 18 Feb. 1994.
2. The translation is Michael Stanislawski's from his definitive biography of Y.L. Gordon *For Whom Do I Toil? Judah Leib Gordon and the Crisis of Russian Jewry* (Oxford: Oxford University Press, 1988), pp.104–5.
3. S. Halkin, *Trends and Forms in Modern Hebrew Literature* (Jerusalem: Mossad Bialik, 1984), pp.14–21.
4. See Yedidiyah Yitshaki's article 'Sifrut Haya be'lashon Meta' [A Living Literature in a Dead Language], *Criticism and Interpretation*, Bar-Ilan University Press, vol. 25 (April 1989), pp.89–100.
5. In Yaakov Shavit's work, *Poetry and Ideology* (Tel Aviv: Hakibbutz Hameuchad, 1987), pp.28–32, an interesting parallel is being drawn between medieval and modern Hebrew poetry, both of which regard the Bible not only as a religious book, but also as a source of aesthetic and linguistic inspiration.
6. Itamar Even-Zohar, *Hasifroot* 3-4 (35-36) (1986), pp.46–54, and *Hasifroot* B2 (1970), pp.286–302.
7. Yoram Bronowski claims that Ben-Yehuda's view that Hebrew was one monolithic language

was one reason why he was successful in turning a mistaken hypothesis into a fact. See *Ha-Aretz*, 5 Jan. 1979, p.18.
8. E. Ben-Yehuda, *Ha-Halom Vesivro* (ed. R. Sivan) (Jerusalem: Sifriyat Dorot, 1978), pp.37–48, and 55–79.
9. Yehuda Amichai, *A Life of Poetry 1948–1994* (New York: Harper Collins, 1994), p.94. The Hebrew version is from *Achshav Bara'ash* (New York: Schocken, 1968), p.38.
10. For the role of Hebrew in the process of cultural and national secularization of Judaism see E. Schweid's analysis in *The Idea of Judaism as a Culture* (Tel Aviv: Am Oved, 1995), pp.293–314.
11. Y.H. Brenner, 'Misaviv Lankooda' [Around the Point], *Hashiloah*, no.14, 1904. Many scholars have analysed the confessional aspect in Brenner's writings, and the link between fiction and reality, but it is beyond the scope of this book to discuss this further.
12. M.Z. Feierberg, *Whither, and Other Stories* (London: The Toby Press, 2004).
13. Benjamin Tammuz, *The Bitter Scent of Geranium* (Tel Aviv: Hakibbutz Hameuchad, [n.d.]), pp.50–62.
14. For more on this see Nurit Zarhi, 'A Journey to the Beginning of the Illusion', *Ha-Aretz*, 25 Jan. 1980, p.16
15. From *Ad Henna* (Tel Aviv: Schocken, 1972), pp.343–95.
16. Gershom Scholem, in a televised conversation with Dan Miron, suggested that the story was based on a book about Ugaritic discoveries. It is interesting to note that during this conversation Scholem confirmed that Agnon wrote the story at Scholem's home in Jerusalem whilst Scholem and his wife were on a visit to the US.
17. All quotes are from the English translation by Walter Lever in *Two Tales by S.Y. Agnon, 'Betrothed' and 'Ido and Enam'* (New York: Schocken, 1996), pp.143–233. The present quotation is from pp.145–6.
18. See more on Agnon's irony in A. Band, *Nostalgia and Nightmare* (Berkeley, CA: University of California Press, 1968), pp.382–96.
19. Most of the characters in this story have first names which begin with the letter 'g', drawing our attention to the ontological value of the letters.
20. Interestingly, Agnon makes a comparison between this and those who rejected settling in Eretz Israel in favour of the good life abroad, Lever, *Two Tales by S.Y. Agnon*, p.372.
21. Lever, *Two Tales by S.Y. Agnon*, pp.160–1.
22. Adi Tsemah, *Fine Lettres, Hebrew Literature of the 20th Century* (Jerusalem: Mossad Bialik, 1990), pp.40–51.
23. The poet Bialik had already warned that 'there is no development and no renewal where there is no tradition to build upon' in his article 'Hasefer Ha'Ivri' in H.N. Bialik, *Kol Kitvei* [All the Writings] (Tel Aviv: Dvir, 1971), p.204. This position is in direct conflict with that adopted by the Age of Revival's Berdichevsky. See his essay in *An Anthology of Hebrew Essays*, selected by Israel Cohen and B.Y. Michali (Jerusalem: Massada, 1966), p.142.
24. For a wide discussion on the subject of Israeli identity, see Robert Wistrich and David Ohana (eds), *The Shaping of Israeli Identity – Myth, Memory and Trauma* (London: Frank Cass, 1996).
25. From 'Forms' by Yona Wallach, *Selected Poems 1963–1985* (Tel Aviv: Hakibbutz Hameuchad, 1992), pp.180–2.
26. Arnold Band, 'Regelson, Pagis, Wallach: Three Poems on the Hebrew Language' in *Solving the Riddles* (1995), p.521.
27. For more on this see Roy Scafer's article, 'On Gendered Discourse and Discourse on Gender', in J.H. Smith and Afaf M. Mahfouz (eds), *Psychoanalysis, Feminism, and the Future of Gender* (Baltimore, MD: Johns Hopkins University Press, 1994), pp.1–21.

3

'Ut Pictura Poesis': The Expression of Ideology in Nathan Shaham's *Series*

The theme of cultural identity, and in particular Jewish and Israeli identity, is an ever-growing preoccupation in Israeli literature. Nathan Shaham's novel *Series*[1] is a typical example, especially in its concern with the search for an appropriate medium through which to express its essentially political ideas.

In recent years, many Israelis have been deeply involved in examining and analysing their national identity, which was shaped by the founders of Israeli nationalism, the early Zionists of the late nineteenth and early twentieth centuries. Early Zionism sought to construct the 'New Jew', whose ethos was to be secular and revolutionary. It was based on a new set of values, on a new (or re-newed) link between the Jew and his ancestral homeland, and on the negation of the exilic existence.[2] Zionist ideology sought to re-define Jewish identity, and thereby rendered ideology and identity inseparable.[3] The Frankfurt School Marxist Theodor Adorno argued against the espousal of an ideology or particular identity, because both 'homogenize' the world, equating distinct phenomena, and suppress all contradiction. According to him, ideology is a 'totalitarian' system which manages and processes all social conflict out of existence, whereas identity is a 'primal form' of all ideology.[4] Only art speaks up for the differential and non-identical, promoting the claims of the sensuous particular against the tyranny of some seamless totality. One could argue against Adorno's critique, as does the critic Terry Eagleton, by pointing out that the real ideological conditions of Western societies are far from being totalitarian, and are mixed and self-contradictory.⁵ However, what is relevant here is that the two opposing sides of this argument both acknowledge that identity and ideology are closely interlinked, as indeed is the case with Zionism.

This argument is presented as one of the central themes in Shaham's novel. It tells of a television crew of three who in 1991, during the Palestinian uprising, or *intifada*,⁶ are engaged in preparing a series of ten documentary programmes for Israeli television.⁷ It is recounted by an omniscient narrator, who in each chapter shifts his vantage point to that of a different character. The principal protagonist, Adam Bauman, aged 40, once a famous Polish film maker, has not made a film since he left for the West, failing both in the United States, his first stop, and in Israel, where he now lives. Having agreed to make the documentary series, he chooses an American, Peter Kelner, aged nearly 50, as camera-man, and the young, Israeli-born Na'ama Sternberg, still in her twenties, as researcher.

Brought up as a true American, Peter wants to choose ten true stories of exceptional characters (p.16). On the other hand Adam, the Pole, wants to tell his story through 'very unimportant people' (p.17), or 'grey' characters, explaining to Peter that he has a 'hidden ambition to succeed where others had failed. Every average director can make an attractive film about big people from life. Only a great director can make an inspiring film about average people and force the spectator to take an interest in their miserable fate.' Famous people bore him. It is not the exceptional who will be the protagonists of his series, but the 'typical' (p.16). He is therefore determined to find ten representative, but ordinary, members of Israeli society and transform them into figures worthy of trust and respect, 'to present in a programme of ten portraits, a slice of colourful Israeli society, and to draw a kind of mosaic of fates all meeting at the focal point of Jewish existence' (p.161). Significantly, this mosaic excluded Oriental Jews even though the series was supposed to represent Adam's perception of the strange condition of Jewish life,⁸ of which Oriental Jews are a considerable element, and indeed, the trio involved in making the film are all of Ashkenazi extraction. (For more on the attitude to Oriental Jews, and on their contribution to Hebrew Literature since the establishment of the State of Israel, see 'The Loneliness of the Wanderers: *Water Touching Water*', pp. 67–77.)

Adam wants the series to embody an idea, to give a history lesson, to portray the anomaly of the Jew (p.18). However, his views are not consolidated. He has no plan for how to go about it, and is hoping that one will emerge in the course of the work itself (p.164). This vague approach is noted critically by Na'ama, who observes that Adam's work, like his private life, is obscure and ambiguous (pp.36–7). Not only does he not have a plan, but he believes that in the preparation of a documentary film, not everything should be planned in advance, 'things which are discovered by chance, whilst filming, can have the most effective result' (p.164). Interestingly, this ambiguity is reflected in the very structure of Shaham's novel itself. Just as Adam hopes to do in the course of filming, the readers of Shaham's novel discover things by chance, and the conversations seem to flow somewhat ambiguously and as if unplanned. The difference between the two is that, whereas Adam never completes his film, Shaham produced a finished work. Adam's excuse is lack of funds, but in fact his courage and confidence have left him (pp.259, 260, 262). He is afraid of failure (p.153). Shaham was not.

Na'ama's official task is to collate archive material for the series, but in practice her main function is to act as a bridge between Adam and Peter and Israel, where they feel themselves to be outsiders (p.107). As Peter says, Na'ama translates his thoughts into the local language. She is 'the window through which he looks out at this dry landscape' (p.186). Na'ama, the only native-born Israeli of the three, knows things about Israel that they do not, not least how to deal with the local bureaucracy. Yet, despite their different views of how to present Jewish and Israeli history, all three of them seek to establish continuity between the past, present and future. They appear to see history as the very means by which identity is shaped and evolves. Their search for the right protagonists for the film is also the catalyst for the three crew members to examine their own individual Jewish identity. In the same way, Shaham invites the readers, in turn, to embark on their own search for identity.

The crew first considers telling the story of Peter's friend, Ron Sharp from Nebraska. Born to a Jewish mother and a Christian father, he grew up as a Christian, married a Jewess as his father had done and served in the American marines. He was wounded in Vietnam and was currently studying as a convert in a Yeshiva in Hebron (p.43). He was involved with the settlement of the West Bank and was suspected of killing an Arab boy. Although Peter thinks him a suitable candidate for the series, Adam rejects him as a subject because he does not want to mix art with politics (and naively believes he can keep the two separate). This may well have been a reaction to his upbringing, which supported the Marxist approach to engaged art, the mixing of art with politics. He is also cautious and does not want to be politically identified with right-wing Jewish settlers of the West Bank, nor involved in controversial issues (pp.124, 163).

Another candidate is a 78-year-old Kibbutz member, potentially a representative of the success of the secular 'New Hebrew' in Israel.

However, ironically, Adam regards his story as too perfect to be authentic. His personal sacrifices for his country and his heroism during the fight for Israel's independence have become a myth. This superhuman devotion is not what the series is supposed to represent (pp.238–9). Next is Na'ama's family friend Bet-El, who believes in the importance of ancient Hebrew as the link between Jewish history and religion (p.115). But she also fails to match Adam's preconceived concept of a 'typical' Jew. Finally, 75-year-old Dr Zilber is chosen. She is a Holocaust survivor, whose past had been taken from her (as she says: 'no contemporary Eastern European Jew had a family album'), and who works as a volunteer with Arab women in Northern Israel – surprisingly, since the novel was published in 1992, during the Intifada, when relationships between Arabs and Israelis were particularly tense. Her dramatic life corresponds to Adam's – and clearly Shaham's – idea of the 'typical' abnormality of Jewish life.

The crew's debate over who to choose as typical and atypical is loaded with irony in that the crew itself exemplifies and is a microcosm of the problem, being made up of uprooted misfits and 'typically atypical' types. Like the crew, and the candidates, Israeli society is made up of atypical individuals, the casualties of a Jewish history which prevented the Jew from developing 'normally', or to pattern. The issue raises ideas concerning the rhetoric of iconoclasm, and alludes to the debate over Marxism and ideology. It appears that Adam cannot free himself from the Marxist approach to representation, in that he wants his characters to be representative, or as Marx would say, to serve as the image behind the concept, the *camera obscura*, or 'dark room' in which images are projected. The characters would be used not only as concrete vehicles, but as metaphors for abstract ideas. Adam's approach is particularly difficult because of his awareness of the crippling effect of concrete concepts. He wants the characters to be 'historically situated figures that carry a political unconscious along with them'. Such figures are, as W.J.T. Mitchell the leading post-structuralist scholar cites, based on what Adorno and the Frankfurt school called 'dialectical images', 'crystallizations of the historical process' or 'objective constellations in which the social condition represents itself ... We need to realize that ... the essence of the dialectical image is its polyvalence – as object in the world, as representation, as analytical tool, as historical device, as figure – most of all as a Janus-faced emblem of our predicament, a mirror of history, and a window beyond it.'[9] Because of Adam's awareness of the complexity of the rhetoric of iconoclasm, he struggles to find a suitable way to represent his ideas, and thus choose characters, for his television series.

Irving Howe's comments about the political writer, apply equally to Adam, the film maker:

> The ideas of actual life, which may have prompted the writer to compose his novel, must be left inviolate; the novelist has no business tampering with them in their own domain, nor does he generally have the qualifications for doing so. But once these ideas are set to work within the novel they cannot long remain mere lumps of abstraction ... This is one of the great problems, but also one of the supreme challenges, for the political novelist to make ideas or ideologies come to life, to endow them with the capacity for stirring characters into passionate gestures and sacrifices, and even more, to create the illusion that they have a kind of independent motion, so that they themselves – those abstract weights of idea or ideology – seem to become active characters in the political novel.[10]

Alongside the struggle to find the 'right' protagonist, Adam also agonizes over the appropriateness of television as a medium for expressing such difficult issues as religion, displacement and identity. The problems of presentation of such ideological and abstract ideas in an artistic medium also preoccupy Shaham. Both, one in the form of images and the other in verbal form, are attempting to get to the heart of human experience at its most private, but they do so whilst the direction in which the emotion moves, the weight it exerts, are all conditioned, or controlled by the pressure of abstract thought. They both have to handle several themes at once and to find a way in which ideas in the work of art are transformed into something other than the ideas of a political programme. In addition, filmic images, like writing, are representational. But whereas Shaham is clearly aware of this distancing from pure objectivity, it seems that Adam, just like Peter, fails to accept the 'disturbance' of photography, and its cunning ability to dissociate consciousness from identity. It is the advent of oneself as 'other', the 'disturbance' which Roland Barthes observed, that transforms subject into object.[11]

The seductiveness of the visual image is a well-established preoccupation of Shaham's. Through his involvement in film-making he helped to establish Israeli television in 1967, but ultimately came to the conclusion that television might have an adverse effect on viewers, and warned: 'I am worried about the fact that we speak in pictures, that we raise a generation who believes that what they see in pictures is the absolute truth'.[12] Shaham expresses these concerns in *Series* through Adam. He raises such basic questions as: can a television film be considered a form of art? Is a film maker answerable to moral criteria?

What is the nature of the link between television and literature? Can one represent the truth in any form of art? Is the word superior to the image? W.J.T. Mitchell addresses many of these questions in his study on image, text and ideology,[13] and as far as the question of the superiority of word over image is concerned, he suggests:

> the relationship between words and images reflects, within the realm of representation, signification, and communication, the relations we posit between symbols and the world, signs and their meanings. We imagine the gulf between words and images to be as wide as the one between words and things ... I propose ... that we treat it ... as a struggle that carries the fundamental contradictions of our culture into the heart of theoretical discourse itself. The point, then, is not to heal the split between words and images, but to see what interests and powers it serves.[14]

Shaham's view on this subject, as represented in this novel, is different. He is using this argument as a rhetorical prism through which to examine Israeli ideology and Jewish identity. He had done this in his earlier novel, *The Rosendorf Quartet* (1987), in which he explored the link between words and music. In *Series* he instead compares words with pictures, ultimately reaching the conclusion that words are the more truthful of the two media. And like *The Rosendorf Quartet*, *Series* is also a microcosm of the Jewish people and its tumultuous destiny.[15] It is essentially an ideological novel, combining major political and historical issues with observations on the artistic media available to examine these issues.[16]

The debate over medium, that is, image versus text, has exercised commentators since word and image existed and has gained a new poignancy since the cultural invasion of the television. It seems relevant to survey briefly its history as this is one of the two pivots around which the novel revolves. The debate has its roots in ancient classical thought. In his *Ut Pictura Poesis* Horace was one of the first commentators to make a case for minimizing the differences between all forms of art, particularly painting and poetry. During the Italian Renaissance, however, Leonardo da Vinci clearly saw the two as very different, even opposing, forms of expression, and sought to elevate painting to a higher level than poetry, claiming that painting is a more universal art form as it does not rely on the mediation of words. However, by the eighteenth century, plastic art, music, theatre and poetry were accorded equal status, following John Dryden's coinage in 1695, 'The Sister Arts'.[17] During the nineteenth century, comparison between the arts was not a fashionable preoccupation. It was not until the turn of the twentieth century that it again became an issue for furious debate.[18] During the early part of the twentieth century, there was a tendency towards blurring any distinction between the arts, concentrating instead on finding analogies between the different media. Contemporary scholarship, however, is engaged in exploring the interaction between 'Ut Pictura' and 'Poesis', the visual and the verbal, from a new perspective. It is not only preoccupied with the supremacy of one form over another, but is also engaged at a more fundamental level, questioning the conventional view that different forms of art exist separately and independently of each other and that any comparison between the arts can only be based on a binary system of analogies.[19]

The fundamental assumption of the separateness of each form of art on which the concept of comparison and analogy depends[20] was overturned in the middle of the century by W.J.T. Mitchell. He sees the division of the terrain of 'Word and Image', between film, television and the book as more complicated than simply a question of supremacy or greater purity. For him, there is no essential difference between poetry and picture: they cannot be compared with one another as they are part of the same phenomenon, reaching perhaps their ultimate expression in television, in which images, sound and words 'flow' into one another. According to this view, every form of art incorporates another medium, and all can co-exist in one form of art.[21] All media are mixed media, and all representations are heterogenous. He opposes the compulsion to conceive of the relation between words and images in political terms, as a struggle for territory, a contest of rival ideologies, and points out that in contemporary culture the visual presentation is once again struggling for hegemony over verbal discourse. Changing modes of representation and communication, thanks largely to the advent of film, television and the computer, are altering the very structure of human experience. We live in a culture governed by the supremacy of the visual, a society that believes what it sees and upholds the validity of superficial appearance, or form, over content. Shaham argues here against this view by having his protagonists' film struggle then fail.

Shaham is also preoccupied with the question of the ideological power behind basic aesthetic issues such as that of representation. Politics and ideology are deeply connected with issues of representation and medium, and the use of the media in attaining and maintaining political power.[22] We are assaulted by both visual and verbal propaganda in which the issues have become subservient to the manner of their expression. In his essay on the work of art in the age of mechanical reproduction, Walter Benjamin pointed out that film reveals the immense new field of action. It can have revolutionary functions, and is able to mobilize the masses.²³ It is no longer possible (if indeed it ever were) to tease out the ideology from the aesthetic: politics and presentation are more than ever inextricably linked and cannot easily be separated out.

These issues are addressed head-on in *Series*. Adam believes that presenting the truth should be the only pursuit of cinematic art. In this respect he regards it as superior to any other form of art (p.23) and says: 'one picture weighs more than a thousand words'(p.66). Words take away the mystery, whereas the camera can give many meanings (p.6). According to him, being a very plastic medium, the picture can change its meaning when linked with pictures from a different context (p.41). Adam believes that 'pictures are better than words to show loneliness, emptiness, desolation, despair and disappointment, even bereavement' (p.71). Film 'tells a story, paints a picture, adds a deep dimension to everyday dialogue. It contains rhythm as music does, it uses symbols and metaphors as in poetry and philosophy ... The cinema brought back the human voice to its natural register' (p.47). Dr Zilber is of the old generation, representing the opposite view, claiming that the use of horrific pictures is banal, debasing events such as the Holocaust. She is unable to accept the modern view that pictures can shape thoughts in the way that words do (p.42): 'a picture can mislead. Without words we cannot know anything' (p.66). Nevertheless, 'Words can also mislead if you do not say everything' (p.69). She is aware of the limitations of language to convey the reality of experience: 'many people, through lack of talent, write books full of facts and events which had great depth in life itself, but become shallow and full of banal empty phrases when written' (p.75). Torn between word and image, yet wanting to tell her story, she consents to appear in the first programme of the series.

Dr Zilber's story raises questions of belief, life in Israel and the Diaspora, Jewish history, Zionism, faith and Jewish and Israeli identity – all of which are major ideological issues in any aesthetic genre, whether verbal or visual. Through the long discussions about the form the series should be shaped into, Shaham draws our attention to the fact that he too, in his novel, is searching for a successful linguistic medium in which to explore these very same topics. He also addresses both directly and indirectly the tension between ideology and art in whatever medium. Ideology is abstract and we are aware that in the most favourable circumstances it is never easily incorporated into a novel. The study of the verbal art can and must overcome the divorce between an abstract 'formal' or purely textual approach and an equally abstract 'ideological' or contextual approach. Shaham's text endorses Irving Howe's observation: 'The conflict is inescapable: the novel tries to confront experience in its immediacy and closeness, while ideology is by its nature general and inclusive.'[24] Yet it is precisely from this conflict that *Series* gains its interest and takes on the aura of high drama.

Acknowledging directly and indirectly the imperfections of the various media available, Shaham nevertheless presents in this novel central issues preoccupying Israeli society. And inevitably, in Israel, every path leads to religion: Na'ama's father repeatedly says that he would have preferred her to deal with media other than film (p.112), invoking the Bible to remind her of the prohibition against statues and false idols. Being an orthodox Jew, he is an advocate of the supremacy of the word over image (p.113). Na'ama clashes with her parents over her involvement in the film, ultimately leaving orthodoxy because she cannot find in religion the two most important things to her: love and liberty (p.26). She can never persuade her father that the plastic art is as serious as the written word.

Indeed, the relationship between children, their parents and their roots is another important theme in the novel, a theme which is closely linked with issues of identity. Both Adam and Peter have suffered a breakdown in their relationships with their parents. Their move towards their Jewish roots is a late reaction, possibly a move towards a reconciliation of their earlier resentment and estrangements. Adam rebels against his father's indoctrination of Communism, and Peter against his father's obsessive commitment to the teaching of Hebrew in the United States, and becomes interested in his father's activities only after his death, coming to Israel not through Zionism, but as a kind of atonement for the pain he had caused his father (p.45). Na'ama, on the other hand, has a warm relationship with her parents, despite their differing attitudes to religion. Yet she, like Adam and Peter, is also uprooted, 'and is hovering in space empty of beliefs' (pp.105–6). As historian Anita Shapira notes,[25] the children of the early Zionists were born into the ethos of the 'New Jew', they did not have to undergo any psychological and existential upheaval, and they sought to reinforce their own identity in relation to that of their parents. Only later, when disillusionment set in, did the next generation begin to question *their* own identity in relation to that of their parents. For Na'ama, the identity of exilic Jewry was distant and mythological. This was not the case with Adam and Peter, the new immigrants. They did not have the same experiences, yet they were required to conform in the melting pot of uncompromising Zionism. Through the discussion on text and image, Shaham puts under scrutiny this ideology, in which the needs of the collective come before the needs of the individual, and raises some fundamental questions: Was not the price the early Zionists had to pay too high?[26] Were the children to be blamed for turning their backs on their fathers' ideology? And most importantly, how can Zionism be reconciled with its Jewish component? Shaham warns of the dangers to both Israeli identity and Jewish existence of the lack in Israeli society of the Jewish element and the Hebrew language, which is a central component of Jewish culture.[27] (See also pp.16–17.)

The intimate link between the Hebrew language and the identity of the Jewish people is well established. We are constantly reminded in the book that the common language for the characters is not Hebrew, but English. This draws the reader's attention to the medium of language as a means of communication and as a way of identifying with – or becoming distanced from – culture. Here, language also emphasizes the protagonists' distance from Jewish roots. After seven years in Israel Adam still prefers to express himself in English, even though it is not his mother tongue (for example, pp.10, 21, 23, 24, 33, 259). Both he and Peter make mistakes in Hebrew (for example, pp.15, 24, 27, 36, 38, 98, 103, 172). Similarly, Dr Zilber's adopted daughter, Tamara, speaks terrible Hebrew, and much of the time uses Russian (pp.86, 223, 224, 232, 233, 291, 308). Dr Zilber herself speaks mostly in Russian (pp.50, 53, 56, 59, 60), as her Hebrew is very poor and ungrammatical (pp.207, 210).

Language has played an important role in the rise of European nationalism and is particularly relevant to the study of Israeli nationalism. The history of any language is part of political, economic and social history, and particularly so in the case of the Hebrew language. Israel is a country of immigrants who were expected to conform to Zionist ideas and to erase their previous cultural identity. No outsiderness was accepted. Other than Na'ama, none of the characters in *Series* can really call Israel their homeland. Dr Zilber, who lost her two babies in the war, who escaped a concentration camp and was tortured by the Russians, arrived in Israel not because of Zionism, but admits that only anti-Semitism made her Jewish. The question of what makes one Jewish also engages Adam and Peter. Adam defines a Jew as 'someone who was forced to choose a new homeland without ceasing to love his old homeland ... whoever was not exiled, did not wander and choose a place under the sun is not a real Jew'(p.39). According to this definition he is a Jew: he ran away from a Marxist regime which threatened the artist's integrity, and from the superficiality of the New World. Neither offers him a fertile ground for ideological expression. He was promised that at least in Israel he would become part of a whole, not only part of his own generation but of the continuum of all future generations. But, both he and Peter find it hard to put this idea into practice, as they have no Jewish background. Their outsiderness is also a useful narrative device in spotlighting the issues under consideration. It provides a vantage point which enables the onlooker to see a clearer picture of the whole 'inside' and to compare it with the 'outside'.[28] Many Israeli writers today situate their protagonists between home and abroad in their search to redefine Israeli identity (see also pp.4 and 90), and although the distance in Shaham's novel is not physical, it is very much part of the main protagonists' psyches. Most come from another place.[29] Adam and Peter are unable to integrate and so see things in Israel as outsiders. They do not necessarily consider Israel the modern, secular solution to the definition of Jewish identity either on the personal or on the collective level. Right from the start, Adam excludes being engaged in specifically Israeli issues. For him, Israeli culture is an 'optical mistake', based on the abstract concept of Jewish fate. Indeed, he sees himself as making a series of tales about the fate of the Jews rather than about Israel as such. This distinction proves to be false in the end. The novel suggests that Israel is an inseparable component of Jewish identity.

An encounter with a foreign culture, in this case an Israeli culture, which may be both very close to home emotionally but also in some ways very alien, often leads to a conflict which initiates a complex, dialectical process of discovery and even re-structuring of the self. Shaham's protagonists soon discover that belonging to the Jewish people is not only about acquiring or sharing in a collective memory, but also about issues of territory and language. Adam and Peter cannot access this cultural framework, and this is where the core of the novel lies. The dilemmas and the need for a continuous search are a necessary and inevitable stage. Adam and Peter are Jews, but they are not religious. They have no knowledge of Jewish culture, they do not know Yiddish and their Hebrew is very poor. The emphasis on the protagonists' inability to communicate in Hebrew creates the effect of self-consciousness, and underscores the theme of the search for the appropriate vehicle of expression. (For more on this see also chapters 5 and 6.) It brings to the foreground the implication of narrative and the representational in our strategies of making meaning in our culture.[30] But, above all, the novel, like many other contemporary novels, points out that the Hebrew language must remain a central component of Jewish culture. Learning the language might have helped Adam and Peter find a way out of their outsiderness.

Shaham has not provided ready answers to the important questions which he raises in this novel. On the ideological level, he does not suggest which new direction Zionism might take so as to encompass all members of Israeli society. After all, it is not Zionism that keeps the characters in the novel together. Not even the Hebrew national language. What is it? Jewish fate? Will it continue to bind them? Is it not too vague? Whilst Shaham does not give clear answers, he insists that the actual search for answers is a necessary ongoing process in the attempt to redefine Israeli identity.[31] Novelists committed to ideological themes are not obliged to arrive at ideological solutions. However, there is, as Irving Howe reminds us,

> a strong psychological and even moral need among both writers and readers of novels – which is one reason why novels are not, in any strict sense tragedies – to feel that the rendered situations may not be utterly intractable; that sooner or later there may be a slight motion of change ... the writer can only struggle, through the sobrieties of realism or the artifice of antirealism, hoping to cope with or get round, or best of all, engage once again the urgencies of his moment.[32]

It is also not clear from the novel what new shape Israeli identity will assume. Can it rely for inspiration on the Jewish religious roots of its members in such a way that it will be meaningful to the Israelis, the majority of whom are secular?[33] Perhaps now is the 'plastic hour' as Gershom Scholem called it, the moment in the life of mankind when new possibilities come to light. One thing is clear from the end of the novel, and that is that politics have overridden and overwritten art: Adam and Dr Zilber's adopted daughter are both murdered by Arab terrorists and any plans for producing the programme die with them. Adam, who had not wanted politics to enter the series (pp.20, 163, 252), is, ironically, conquered by politics. The novel thus illustrates that politics and art cannot be separated in real life. The ideological and the aesthetic have turned out to be inseparable. 'Ideology both constructs and is constructed by the way in which we live our role in the social totality.'[34] Perhaps one of the main conclusions the novel draws is that one should not analyse the formal articulation of a genre, be it visual or verbal, independently of its political and ideological address. The tension between ideology and literature is presented here alongside the tension between text and image. Shaham uses a poetic exploration of the relationship between 'Pictura' and 'Poesis' in his quest for the meaning of Jewish history and Israeli identity.

NOTES

1. Nathan Shaham, *Series* (Tel Aviv: Am Oved, 1992). Shaham, born in Tel Aviv in 1925, is the son of the late novelist Eliezer Steinmann. He studied at the renowned Hertzliya High school, and then served in the Palmach (the striking force of the voluntary Jewish self-defence organisation established in Palestine during the British Mandate) and the Israeli army. He has been a member of Kibbutz Bet Alfa since 1945, and a recipient of many prestigious literary prizes.
2. For more on this subject see the Introduction in Anita Shapira, *New Jews Old Jews* (Tel Aviv: Am Oved, 1997), pp.9–17.
3. See, for example, the recent study by Oz Almog, *Hatsabar-Dyokan* [The Sabra: A Profile] (Tel Aviv: Am Oved, 1997).
4. Terry Eagleton, *Ideology* (London: Verso, 1991), p.126, and Theodor Adorno, *Aesthetic Theory* (London: Continuum, 1984).
5. Eagleton, *Ideology*, p.128.
6. *Intifada* is the Palestinian uprising which started in December 1987 and ended in September 1993.
7. For a detailed analysis of this novel see Yosef Oren, *Identities in Israeli Prose* (Rishon Letsion: Yahad, 1994), pp.175–92.
8. It is interesting to note that up to 1967 only one voice was heard in Israeli literature: Ashkenazi, male, socialist, secular and politically identified with the left. Writers represented a false picture of a cohesive society.
9. W.J.T. Mitchell, *Iconology – Image, Text, Ideology* (Chicago: University of Chicago Press, 1987), pp.204–5. For an extensive analysis of the preceding remarks on Marxism, ideology and fetishism see pp.160–208.
10. Irving Howe, *Politics and the Novel* (New York: New American Library, 1987), p.21.
11. Roland Barthes, *Camera Lucida* (London: Vintage, 1993), pp.12–13.
12. Interview with D. Karpal in *Ha-Aretz*, 13 Nov. 1992, pp.42–5.
13. Mitchell, *Iconology – Image, Text, Ideology*, p.44.
14. One should note here that semioticians break down the notion of 'literariness' altogether, and suggest that there is nothing that is not potentially or actually a sign. From this point of view they see no distinction between word and image.
15. For a detailed analysis of this novel see Ziva Shamir, 'Of Poetics and Politics', *Modern Hebrew Literature*, 12 (Tel Aviv University, Spring/Summer 1994), pp.12–14.
16. By an ideological novel I mean a novel in which ideological themes play a major role, and in which the relation between ideology and literature is central. It seems interesting to note that the theory of ideology has been the subject of the liveliest disputes and elaboration in modern Marxist criticism of culture.
17. John Dryden, 'A Parallel of Poetry and Painting', in W.P. Ker (ed.), *Essays of John Dryden* (London, 1900), Vol.II, pp.115–53.
18. I am indebted to the analysis and the rich bibliography on this subject by Avner Holtzman in *Literature and the Visual Arts* (Tel Aviv: Hakibbutz Hameuchad, 1997).
19. For more on this subject, see Raymond Williams, *Television: Technology and Culture Form* (London: Fontana, 1974), p.92.
20. See, for example, Rene Wellek, 'The Parallelism Between Literature and the Arts', in *English Institute Annual* (New York: Columbia University Press, 1942), pp.26–63.
21. W.J.T. Mitchell, *Picture Theory* (Chicago and London: University of Chicago Press, 1994), pp.94–5. Also: Mitchell, *Iconology – Image, Text, Ideology*, p.49.
22. See Mitchell, *Picture Theory*, p.1.
23. Walter Benjamin, *Illuminations* (London: Fontana/Collins, 1979), pp.219–44.
24. Howe, *Politics and the Novel*, p.20.
25. Shapira, *New Jews Old Jews*, p.12.
26. Benjamin Tammuz raised similar questions in his short story 'The Bitter Scent of Geranium', from *The Bitter Scent of Geranium* (Tel Aviv: Hakibbutz Hameuchad, [n.d.]), pp.50–62.
27. In the novellas included in *The Streets of Ashkelon* (Tel Aviv: Am Oved, 1985), Shaham is critical of the lack of Jewish education in the life of American Jews. He examines the meaning of Jewish existence and questions the possibility of its continuation. Even secular Israelis have started to worry that by giving up biblical heroism, they may lose their right to the land. Shaham, *Series*, p.259.
28. See also, Risa Domb, *Home Thoughts From Abroad: Distant Visions of Israel in*

Contemporary Hebrew Fiction (London and Portland, OR: Vallentine Mitchell, 1995), p.6.
29. It is interesting to note that the inside/outside dichotomy introduced a thematic opposition in Hebrew literature as early as the Age of Enlightenment, when any presentation of inside/outside would automatically be taken as relating to the conflict between Jewish values and secular European values, 'between what lay inside the "camp" or the "home" and what lay beyond it'. See Alan Mintz, *Banished from Their Fathers' Table: Loss of Faith and Hebrew Autobiography* (Bloomington, IN: Indiana University Press, 1989), p.96.
30. Linda Hutcheon, *A Poetics of Postmodernism: History, Theory, Fiction* (New York and London: Routledge, 1988), p.183.
31. It seems interesting to cite the film-maker Noorit Aviv, who said in an interview with D. Karpal that she too does not give answers to similar questions that she raises in her film *Place, Work*. 'It is important for me to confront identity, especially Israeli identity, which is actually just fiction. What is Israeli? The Israeli exists for only fifty years, and we are talking about people who came from different places around the world.' (*Ha-Aretz* supplement, 28 Aug. 1998, p.45.)
32. Howe, *Politics and the Novel*, p.255.
33. It seems appropriate to cite Kafka here, who on 16 September 1915, the eve of Yom Kippur, noted in his diary: 'Not going to synagogue is an act of suicide'.
34. Hutcheon, *A Poetics of Postmodernism*, p.178.

4

Touching the Pain: Memory and Identity in *The Last Jew* by Yoram Kaniuk

The Last Jew[1] deals with the problematic nature of Jewish identity in an age of unprecedented historical change, with the Holocaust as the central catalyst for that change. The sociologist Stuart Hall said of identities that they are about:

> using the resources of history, language and culture in the process of becoming rather than of being. Identities are therefore constituted within, not outside representation. Precisely because identities are constructed within, not outside discourse, we need to understand them as products of specific historical and institutional sites within specific discursive formations and practices, by specific enunciative strategies.[2]

This general definition is relevant to specifically Israeli identity, and also to Kaniuk's novel.

As secular Israelis move away from original Zionist ideology, so their need to define their identity increases, and *The Last Jew*, which appeared remarkably early in this process of redefinition, attempts to engage both with the process and its outcomes. Needless to say, a work that encompasses so wide a span of history, people and places is bound to resist categorization.[3] Questions such as: Who am I? Where did I come from? Where do I go from here?, which could have been posed by a Jew at almost any time since the Enlightenment, are employed by Kaniuk to challenge fundamental assumptions in Israeli society.[4] Kaniuk acknowledges that he is 'trying something different ... I enter corners where no one has been before ... never choosing the safe route.

Memory and Identity in The Last Jew

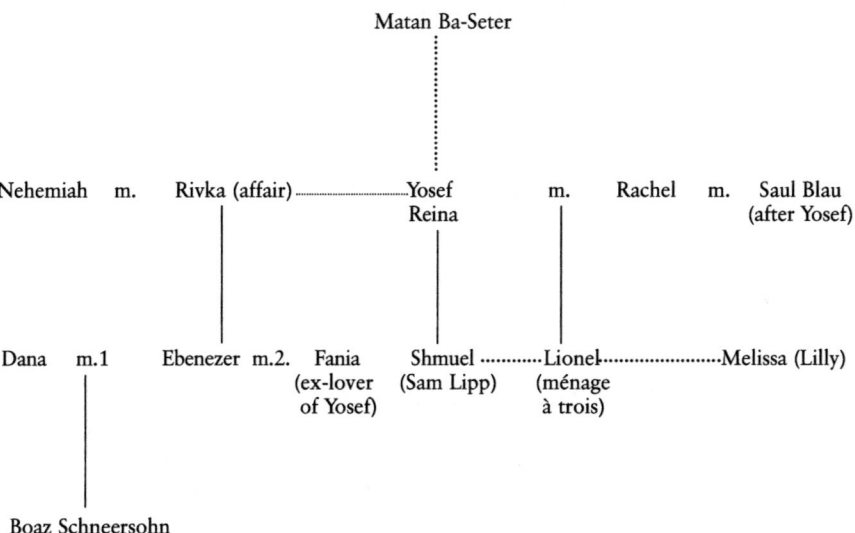

PRINCIPAL RELATIONSHIPS IN *THE LAST JEW*

But I pay dearly ... Israelis don't like people touching the fire like that, touching the pain.'[5]

Critics have written a great deal about *The Last Jew*. Gabriel Moked, said 'that it is one of the most remarkable works of recent Hebrew literature',[6] while Avraham Hagorni, who praises Kaniuk's view of the need to ensure continuity between the Diaspora past and Israeli present, sees in the novel a powerful critique of the early-Zionist rejection of 'Jewishness' in forging a new Israeli identity.[7] 'This great work contains so much material and such brilliance that it is more a study ... than an entertainment',[8] comments one critic. Others who are impressed by the book include Mordechai Fechter, Avraham Oz and M. Avishai.[9] On the other hand, critics such as Baruch Kurtzweil, Avraham Blatt, Yosef Alroi, Sh. Srayah and Yosef Hagorni have been less impressed. Many point to Kaniuk's excessively baroque use of 'words, words, words',[10] fluctuating between high and low registers, that 'tire the reader, but even more so the narrator, and lead to some failures'.[11] No doubt a good editorial hand might have made it more accessible.[12] The account of Krammer (pp.85–108), the description of the battle of Jerusalem (pp.238–9), the tale of Kavidius the Wanderer (p.284)[13] and the description of the mortuary (p.305),[14] among others, would all have lent themselves well to separate stories.

Since the elements of the novel are apparently disconnected in time and place, an annotated summary, however discontinuous the narrative is, is vital as a framework for discussion. In the opening pages the protagonist, referred to merely as 'the young man', seems unsure of his identity, has lost his memory and is apparently in a state of shock (for example, pp.10, 17, 18, 19). A chance meeting with a woman who knows him reveals – to him and the reader – that his name is Boaz, but the narrative continues to be destabilized by the recurrence of 'perhaps', 'possibly' and irrational juxtapositions of cause and effect linked by the word 'therefore' (for example, pp.14, 15). The sense of time is confused and it takes four pages to determine that the events described are taking place during the 1948 War of Independence, soon after the State had been established and rationing and blackout imposed (pp.11, 14, 21, 25). Boaz makes his way to the 'office for redirecting soldiers who had left their units through no fault of their own' in Tel Aviv, where he discovers how his unit had been ambushed during one of the fiercest battles at Har'el in the Jerusalem hills, and out of thirty-two only he and two others survived. 'Boaz Schneersohn lay among the dead, pretending also to be dead. Two or three hundred times he was condemned to death, since each shot fired at the dead could have killed him. Which is perhaps how the image of a vulture imprinted itself on his brain' (pp.334–5). Kaniuk himself had lived through such an experience, which he describes as 'not like war, not like battle. Unlike anything. You lie, must not move, and you know you are going to die, but you do not die. All my stories, everything I have written since then, has been connected with this story.'[15]

Boaz meets a 'young man', identical to him but surrounded by an aureole, who mentions that, like Boaz, he had been sent to fight in the Jerusalem hills, in his case only two days after his arrival in Palestine from Europe. He had also survived by pretending to be dead (pp.208–9), and from then on 'it is not clear who is who' (p.24), for this second 'young man', probably Shmuel Lipker, later Sam Lip, and probably Boaz's uncle, functions as Boaz's alter ego, and the pair are like 'two sides of the same coin' (pp.83–4). Boaz's family history through several generations emerges slowly and with some lack of chronological and historical clarity. His father, Ebenezer, a child of one of the new settlements in early twentieth-century Palestine, finds himself in Europe at the outbreak of the Second World War looking for the man he believes to be his biological father, Yosef Reina. Yosef is a descendent of Matan Ba-Seter,[16] a mystic who follows the false messiah, Jacob Frank (a historical figure of the eighteenth century) into Christianity and joins a monastic Order. (False messiahs appear elsewhere in this novel – for example, on pp.113, 117, 120 – forming a suggestive sub-theme.)[17] Both Matan Ba-Seter, who later turns to Marxism and is eventually hanged as a revolutionary, and his wife are depicted on a mythic scale and both eventually go mad (pp.120–1).

After his mother's death Yosef wanders Europe, is said to have fathered fifty-two children (p.123), spends 1897 in the Holy Land with his Danish lover and returns to Europe to compose poems about the Land of Israel that later become famous (p.125).

Yosef marries Rachel Brin, but during the wedding festivities falls in love with Rivka, her best friend, with whom he makes love for three days with Rachel's knowledge (p.132). He is eventually shot at Dachau aged 62 (p.182). By the time Rivka gives birth to Ebenezer she has married a Zionist leader, Nehemiah Schneersohn, whose family name is probably not coincidentally also that of a dynasty of Hasidic rabbis. They leave for Palestine even though her preference is to go to America. The names Rivka and Yosef echo those of brother and sister, Rivka and Joseph Della Reina – the latter a legendary precursor of messianic redemption – who appear in Kaniuk's earlier works *Aunt Shlomtsion the Queen* and *The Death of a Donkey*.[18] On 1 January 1900 Nehemiah and Rivka, with a small group of other pioneers, establish a settlement near the Arab village of Merar (p.147), Nehemiah wishing 'to rebuild the kingdom of David and Solomon, to raise Jephthahs and Boazes and nurture no more prophets' (p.129). Their lack of agricultural experience causes their crops to fail and they suffer from the hostility of Baron de Rothschild's administrators (for example, p.152) and the corruption of Turkish rule (for example, p.153). Rivka weeps for eight years and leaves her son, Ebenezer, whom she is unable to love, to be raised by an Arab woman, there being no reference at this stage in the novel to Arab hostility. Lonely and bored at school, when he is 8 years old the boy discovers how to carve in wood, causing Rivka to lament that 'the Hebrew hero who should have grown up happily on the ancestral soil has instead become a carpenter, just like this stupid [Arab] carpenter from Jaffa' (p.157). Nehemiah realizes that he cannot overcome Rivka's longing for America, that he has failed to gain her love, that Palestine is to her 'an alien land' (p.157) and that she cannot forgive the pioneers, whom she compares to 'beggars dreaming about a kingdom' (p.381), for 'the impertinence that nurtured longings in them as if this place had not died thousands of years ago' (p.141). After nine years in the settlement Nehemiah agrees to leave for America leaving Ebenezer behind, and instals Rivka on board ship in Jaffa harbour before committing suicide on the shore. Rivka promptly disembarks and returns to Merar where she establishes a successful farm (for example, p.165), becoming in old age a symbol of successful survival (p.262), an 'ancient castle' (p.372). For forty-five years her only close friend is Captain Goldenberg (p.217), a British officer (p.215) on an obscure mission in Palestine, possibly representing 'an international body, mysterious, perhaps even religious ... whose purpose is to proselytize the Jews of Eretz Israel and prevent the country from becoming a Zionist base' (p.232). He loves and wants to marry her, but for years she allows him to visit her only on Wednesdays (p.325), admitting just before his death to having begun to like him (p.356).

Rivka cannot love her own son, Ebenezer, but is passionate about Boaz, her grandson, claiming him as her own son 'from the moment he was born' (p.230). Ebenezer, strong and strange, 'did not know many words' (p.227), seems innocent, lacks education (p.250) and is regarded by his mother as retarded (for example, pp.214, 221, 231). But equally he is described as a wizard with words, who remembers what one should not remember (for example, pp.82, 85). At the age of 26 he meets and marries Dana, 'the teacher who fell in love with a carpenter' (pp.226, 228), and Boaz is born in 1928, at the very same hour as Shmuel Lipker (p.231), their identities being so confused and merged from the start (p.378) that Shmuel Lipker is also called Boaz Schneersohn (p.405). When Dana is attacked and buried alive by two Arabs (p.235), Ebenezer kills the old man who raped her and leaves for Europe. In a concentration camp in Europe he meets Shmuel, not realizing he is possibly Yosef Reina's son (p.168), although, ambiguously, we are also told that 'Shmuel's father did not know that Shmuel was not his son' (p.183). Shmuel is the result of an almost ridiculous coupling between Yosef and a woman who spends her life in a locked room acting out the part of her favourite heroines, and his strange origins confer on him a kind of mythic or mystical status. When the camp is liberated (pp.169, 172), Ebenezer meets Fania in a mental hospital in Germany and in 1958 they marry (p.250). She had been one of his father, Yosef Reina's lovers, and had a twin who was killed by Mengele (p.249). After forty years away (echoing the Israelites' wilderness years), Ebenezer returns to Israel, which he thought had been conquered, believing as a consequence that 'all the world is German' (p.97). His mother, Rivka dies, at the age of 100, on 7 Adar, the legendary anniversary of Moses's death (p.459). Meanwhile, Rachel Brin, Yosef Reina's jilted bride, has left for America (p.184), seeking 'the trees dripping with gold' that her friend Rivka had told her to expect, and there marries Saul Blau (a play on the name of the writer Saul Bellow) (p.291) who, although he bears the name of a biblical king, is merely 'the king of shirts' (p.291). Rachel Brin's son by Yosef Reina, Lionel, who later volunteers to serve in the British Army in Europe during the Second World War and is decorated (pp.185–6), falls in love when younger with Melissa, a spoilt but neglected

American child who dies of a minor illness possibly through her parents' inattention. Her presence, although it is felt constantly, is vague. As one of the characters, a German writer referred to in the narrative as 'Germanwriter', remarks: 'Melissa is intertwined somehow in this story, but I do not understand how' (pp.404–5).[19]

In Germany after the War Lionel becomes the first lover of Lilly, a local girl twenty years his junior who wants to identify through him with the sufferings of the Jews (p.189) especially those in concentration camps (p.201). Lionel and Lilly live in a ménage à trois with Shmuel, the 23-year-old Sam Lip, whom Ebenezer had met in the camp and Lionel later encounters during the liberation (pp.302–3), and who imagines sleeping with Lilly and stroking Lionel's hair (p.202). They know, although she does not, that they have the same father (p.393). All three move to New York, where Sam studies theatre, concentrating on the Holocaust, which for him takes the form of 'dark and debased rituals performed on lit-up stages' (p.310). He directs a production which includes thousands of pairs of shoes (p.311), trying to construct a fourth Reich (p.395) and blending his narrative with the tale of Joseph Della Reina. Sam's identification with Lionel, somewhat bizarrely leads him to confront Melissa's ageing parents with their responsibility for her death (pp.296–7).

Boaz finally establishes a publishing company, producing hundreds of memorial books, and he also erects and maintains memorials and organizes memorial ceremonies for fallen soldiers, underground heroes, Holocaust victims and ghetto fighters (pp.288, 320). His story is intertwined with that of both his friend Menahem, who survives the same battle in the Jerusalem hills, but who falls fighting for the Old City of Jerusalem (p.238), and of Menahem's father, Obadiah Hankin (usually referred to as Hankin), who is the main narrator of the later sections of the novel and is the character most realistically and consistently portrayed.

In the opening scene of the novel, Boaz is trying in vain to contact Hankin in order to tell him about his son's death. Hankin, the rational 'Zionist-Realist' (p.47) who teaches Hebrew language and literature in a school of which he later becomes headmaster, has a fraught relationship with his wife (for example, pp.51, 57), later offering a home to Menahem's girlfriend Noga – although she is only ambivalently so since they separate weeks before his death (p.237). Hankin first appears in the novel as a member of the Committee for Bereaved Parents, which meets regularly at one of the members' homes, organizing social gatherings, talks and day trips to the Golan, Sinai, Jerusalem and the air bases 'where major battles took place' (for example, pp.56–7). Vivid descriptions of fighting in the War of Independence (for example, p.25) and 1967 (pp.352–3) are juxtaposed with sardonic accounts of parents' meetings, reflecting the writer's contempt for the mythologizing of memories. The core of the novel, based on tapes[20] and letters,[21] is often confusing and unreliable,[22] interspersed with 'apparently', 'probably' and 'I do not know', much like the opening account of Boaz's trip to Tel Aviv.[23] The narrators have knowledge of the future, mentioning, for instance, 'eleven brothers and sisters, but eventually more' (p.114), the fact that someone 'would later arrive in Providence Rhode Island' (p.115) and even that 'Ebenezer, years later, will be the Last Jew' (p.227).

The character known as Germanwriter, a former Nazi official whom Hankin meets at one of the bereaved parents' meetings (and whose name probably alludes to Gunter Grass), writes a book 'that does not want to be written' (p.168), is seen tape-recording its third draft (p.168) and saying that for him words are banal. Later he laments over 'these thousands of pages! Will I be able to weave them into a book?' (p.450). When he finishes he wants to write about absurdity and death (p.182). His life as a writer is not wholly frustrating, however, for his novella entitled *The Beautiful Life of Christina Herzog* is published in New York (p.388), where the German attaché is called Christina. Germanwriter's view of life is contrasted with Sam's of the Holocaust, for while in New York he sees Sam's play about the Holocaust and Joseph Della Reina, set both in the 1940s and in the sixteenth century, but cannot describe it in words any more than he can the scent of a rose. This failure of perception also affects Sam and Lionel, since Lilly complains to Renata, Germanwriter's wife, that neither of 'these two poets, the great-great-grandchildren of messiahs', sees her as flesh and blood (p.204). Sam wonders if the energy spent on writing and re-writing the horrors of the Holocaust is worthwhile, or 'was it all not turning into a book of tears that the Jews hide in cellars?' (p.312). Hankin, a writer who in 1922 publishes his research into Joseph Della Reina (p.65), becomes in turn the writer of a text entitled 'The Last Jew'. This describes a character he hears about from the paralysed tenant of his former colleague, and about whom he starts to write ritually, like a religious scribe merged with a scholar, beginning with a title page that reads: 'The Last Jew – an investigation by Obadiah Hankin' (p.32). The lastness of this Jew is only relative, however; Ebenezer ceases to be the Last Jew when he helps Hankin mend cupboards in his neglected house (p.320), and in the process loses his separateness, becoming just an ordinary old man (p.451). Several male characters in the novel attempt to write, in some cases for profit,[24] while Rivka, interestingly the only woman among them, tries but fails. Boaz publishes memorial books for the fallen, Sam writes plays, Captain Goldenberg keeps diaries, while Mr Klumin sends the High Commissioner a 600-page letter (p.232) and, with Germanwriter, writes a book entitled, like the one in the reader's hand, *The Last Jew* (p.363).[25] Lionel writes a novel that has been turned down by every publisher (p.187) and which he admits has been through six drafts (p.398). Hankin writes about the dead (p.384), but realizes, again like Kaniuk, that 'people will not read or buy' such a book (p.182), mainly because 'the story cannot be divided' (p.56). This self-referential comment reminds us of the problem of this novel itself, which also cannot be broken down into a narrative sequence, as the introductory inventory of titles suggests. Following the publication of his autobiographical *Post Mortem* in 1995, Kaniuk explained in an interview how, for him, 'writing is a painful and wicked revenge. Both suicide and love combined. You write only about the writer ... within the framework of biographies that one changes and converts ... the reader half writes the book.'[26] His experience feeds his fiction, Kaniuk's mother becoming 'a funny mythological character' in *Aunt Shlomtsion the Queen* because, as he has Hankin explain in this novel, 'writing is an attempt to decipher, to discover connections' (p.27), and 'great literature should give birth to things which were not yet born' (p.46). Germanwriter adds that 'to create something big is to touch the aching nerves ... to call for confrontation, to change the world' (p.400). The task is not always conscious, so that 'it is worth asking the characters about the writer, but not the writer about the characters' (p.401).

The reader first encounters, on the half-title page, a narratorial attempt to indicate – or to discount the possibility of finalizing – the structure of the novel. The brief paragraph listing the contents of the novel, hitherto neglected by critics, reads: 'The Teacher Hankin and the Vulture; The Events [or possibly 'Words'] of the Last Jew; Boaz and Shmuel; A Terrible Tale of Yosef and his Descendants; Matan Ba-Seter; The History of the Settlement; All These Wars; The End of the History of the Jews'. But these are arranged not in tabular form as they would be on a conventional contents page, but as continuous prose, and they lack page references. Moreover, the novel is not actually divided according to these subtitles, which merely point to themes. Hankin observes its similarity to life itself: 'life cannot be divided into separate periods, everything is made in one piece' (p.56).

The identity of the narrator is unclear and shifting, the opening pages of the novel being a third-person stream of consciousness, the first-person singular 'I' appearing first on page 21, and the narration subsequently switching back and forth between the third person (for example, p.56) and the first person for the transcription of Hankin's tape. This has the effect of suggesting that the stories of individual Jews are actually all part of the same story, lived – and told – over and over, and differing only with the teller of the tale. This impression is compounded by the seemingly continuous motion of the characters, their rootlessness and their strange interconnectedness across time and place, cumulatively building to suggest a kind of inevitable, deep-rooted and perhaps irreversible condition of the Jewish people as a whole.

Alongside a meandering plot, with bizarre and inexplicable juxtapositions of characters and events, Kaniuk uses language to achieve, according to Shaked, 'a high degree of stylistic expressiveness through the use of unwieldy metaphors and repeated sentences. In terms of vocabulary, his stylistic register seems low, but stylistic intensification is achieved by surprising combinations of heterogeneous elements that produce effects that are not necessarily felicitous.'[27] His baroquely overloaded blends of comic and tragic styles, and the mythic and fantastic,[28] include invented words, often formed by conflating two others, such as *aharkach* (the-time-after-this), *einbnotav* [has-no-daughter], *avshakool* (bereaved-father), *avkapdan* (strict father) and *Germanisofer* (German-writer), giving a kind of mythic or universal status to the thing described. Elsewhere, he captures with remarkable realism and some sarcasm Fania's broken Hebrew (for example, p.385).[29] Rituals and leitmotifs play a significant part, especially birds[30] and dogs,[31] which deserve a separate study, as well as the handing over of a glass of water (for example, pp.27, 31, 116, 244) and Dante's *Divine Comedy* (for example, pp.277, 412, 439), in which hell is 'human and delicate' compared to the vision of hell of the Last Jew (p.453). The vulture appears frequently: it is one of the terms applied to the war in which Boaz and Menahem participate (pp.335, 361, 366). Boaz captures a vulture in the desert (p.385) and himself turns out to be a metaphorical vulture, living off the dead. Hankin, Germanwriter and Ebenezer are all described as vultures at one time or another. The dog, viewed negatively in the Bible, but as a symbol of loyalty, courage, fertility and sexuality in other cultures,[32] appears in an earlier work of Kaniuk's, *Adam the Son of a Dog*, in which he describes how Adam becomes a dog when he cannot face the cruelty of life.[33] In *The Last Jew* the Jews are often described as having a dog's life, and Ebenezer is described as Krammer's dog (p.85) and is horrifically beaten (p.91).

Many of Kaniuk's characters have names with biblical or other associations. Boaz, the male hero of the biblical book of Ruth, is identified in the closing verses as the ancestor of King David, in turn the supposed precursor of the messiah – a frequently recurring theme of Kaniuk's. Other names have already been used in previous works, Nehemiah having been the name of Shlomtsion's husband in *Aunt Shlomtsion the Queen*, underlining Kaniuk's lack of interest in mimetic-psychological characterization.

The place of Christianity and messianism in the novel[34] has been little discussed, although Shaked points out that several of Kaniuk's protagonists are God's servants, shouldering the cross of history.[35] He notes also that Kaniuk associates the figure of the War of Independence hero less with Isaac, in the account of his binding in Genesis 22, than with the crucifixion, focusing more on the merciful mother who identifies with the suffering son than on the perpetrator father.[36] Related scenes include that in which Rivka, desperate to adopt her grandchild as her son, goes through a strange Christian ceremony in Jaffa (pp.114, 258–9, 260), another in which the young soldier who turns out to be Shmuel/Boaz is described as having an aureole (p.21) and the comparison between Ebenezer's carpentry and Joseph's trade (p.157). The stranger (in this case Germanwriter) can act as a useful device for Israelis to examine their own identity (in much the same way as living abroad can throw a new perspective on a home country, see also pp.32 and 90). According to Nurit Goertz,

> We should bear in mind that in many literary works there is a combination of several kinds of anomalous people and strangers. These works place in the centre all those who society pushed aside, and consolidates them into one. *Himo the king of Jerusalem* is a good example: this describes the War of Independence from the point of view of various unconventional characters: a Christian nun who lives in a monastery in which the war victims are rehabilitated, soldiers of Oriental origin who up to then were not regarded as part of that war, eccentrics who seem the absolute opposite of the familiar war heroes, and other characters who are possibly hallucinations, possibly crazy.[37]

The Last Jew has been seen as a surreal, absurd or fantastic novel, Shaked pointing particularly to its expressionist and confessional aspects,[38] although its 470 pages reflect many other genres also, and the surreal and absurd, when juxtaposed with other genres, may appear less so. For instance, the opening scene of the novel, though dreamlike and surreal on one level, turns out to be a precise description of battle trauma, the apparently bizarre connections Boaz makes perhaps serving to show the dissonance of his interior world. However much he tries to suppress the memory of his experiences, the realities of the outside world press in upon him and trigger flashbacks and strange thoughts: 'He started retreating like somebody who truly dreaded knowing who he was ... Then sights passed before his eyes that he would rather forget and blood poured out of him and he planned the destruction of the house opposite.' Other devices used by Kaniuk to emphasise the surreal include connecting contradictory statements using 'therefore' (for example, pp.14, 15); juxtaposing incongruities such as the beach of the prosperous Herzliah Pituach neighbourhood with sounds of a party in 'The Ghettoes' Fighters Street'; and using outlandish metaphors such as 'Thoughts from nowhere in particular stuck in his mind and a bird built a nest on the kiosk roof' (p.21). In all these ways Kaniuk is showing how 'art perhaps endows legitimacy to the absurd. Existence is absurd. Ebenezer is an absurdity to whom there is no possibility of endowing legitimacy; one can perhaps tell him, but not about him' (p.257). Kaniuk occasionally uses thematic symmetry to illustrate fundamental absurdities, such as the comparison between Boaz's return from war to discover that Merar no longer exists (p.7) and his father Ebenezer's belief, on being liberated from the concentration camp, that Palestine is gone and that he is the Last Jew (p.178): 'Boaz thought for a time he would be the last survivor of his unit, his father thought there would be a kind of a Last Jew' (p.280). Boaz (like Kaniuk himself) hides under the dead in the war as Weiss does elsewhere in the novel p.175), while Boaz tramples over Rivka (p.267) and Hankin over his wife (p.279), and the sons both of Germanwriter (pp.72, 84–5) and Hankin have died.

A source of Kaniuk's dissatisfaction with Realism, Ortsion Bartana suggests, is his adoption of K. Tzenik's dictum that the Holocaust, as a defining event in Jewish history, exists on a different planet. Kaniuk abandoned Realism for the fantastic and the grotesque to produce a 'fantastic anatomy' rather than a conventional novel, the Holocaust emanating as though from the 'genes of a monstrous joke in a world which continuously destroys and renews itself'.[39] Bartana notes how, as in Garcia Marquez's *One Hundred Years of Solitude*, human relationships, both demonic and tragic, are presented through the prism of one family. Kaniuk's protagonists Boaz and Sam coalesce, 'Yosef Reina and Boaz Schneersohn are one person born at different times' (p.265) and Shmuel looks like Yosef Reina (p.290), giving these characters an almost mythical power.[40] Renata and Hasya Masha dance 'as if in a kind of magic ritual' (p.72), an aspect of the novel (explored elsewhere)[41] that emerges typically in the account of how, when Rivka is born with the demon inside her, the sun refuses to rise, a slaughtered cock emerges alive from the fire and the tombstone of Rivka's grandmother, who is similarly associated with magic, witches and Satan (pp.116–17), first cracks and then straightens itself (p.111). But while for Marquez the disintegration results from internal weakness, for Kaniuk it is born out of the confrontation with the Holocaust and the War of Independence, major external catalysts of twentieth-century Jewish existence. Gabriel Moked, for whom *The Last Jew* appears to be a stream of consciousness novel, argues that Kaniuk manages to encompass in it twentieth-century Jewish and Israeli reality by juxtaposing conceptual and emotional surfaces such as bereavement, Eastern European Jewry and Nazism without exaggerating the links between them.[42] Israel Barama, who compares the novel to classical Greek theatre and myth and hears in its multitude of voices a choir, 'laughing and crying and suffering and full of hallucinations', implicitly recognizes the scale and complexity of the issues faced by Kaniuk.[43] The authority of the novel derives from the way the central narrative is depicted through a number of voices, transforming it into a witness statement of which the author is merely a passive recorder.

Kaniuk views history in terms of the War of Independence and the Holocaust.[44] Hankin regards these two events as 'two different disasters, a Jewish catastrophe "over there", and a disaster of the wars in which my son gets killed. From this conjunction come the greatest, most horrific moments of our life, the joining of festivity and nightmare, a fatal illness' (p.41).[45] This view of Jewish history leaves no room for Oriental Jewry, however,[46] and there are only passing references to Jews of Aleppo (p.411) and Iraq (p.452). In one scene near Castel in the Jerusalem hills, while looking for somewhere to erect their Dante memorial, Boaz, Hankin and the Captain stumble across a settlement of Jews from Persia, Bukhara and Afghanistan, whom they regard as strange and unsophisticated (p.346). The single Oriental character in the novel, a Yemenite named Yardena, plays a minor and stereotypical role as a Ministry of Defence official responsible for the care of the bereaved families (pp.414, 457, 467). This is surely a serious flaw in any search for a definition of Israeli and Jewish identity. The Arab-Israeli conflict also plays only a small role, with Arabs appearing either in hostile or, in earlier episodes, subordinate roles. However, it is not without envy that Rivka compares Ebenezer's prolonged absence from home with the stability of the Arab family she employs: 'when you connect Arabs to land, there is someone to rely on' (p.340). Similar views are expressed elsewhere, for example on pp.56, 62 and 74, among others.[47] Kaniuk reported in an interview how his former neighbour, the model for the Last Jew, regarded the Arab-Israeli conflict as a 'dwarf of a war' compared to the Holocaust.[48]

The Holocaust, present throughout the novel as the ultimate

absurdity, shapes the lives of its characters. Kaniuk was not in Europe at that time, but has said: 'I feel ashamed I wasn't there'.[49] Ebenezer survives Auschwitz-Birkenau (pp.178–9), and Germanwriter and Sam try to understand a place 'where the rationale is different' (p.430). Shmuel's parents are made into a lampshade (p.203), the legs of a young girl who has sat bent in the dark for three years become stuck together (p.289) and the representation of hatred and anti-Semitism is chilling (pp.192, 193). But appearances may deceive, for 'Testimony has to be false and thereby describe the truth' (p.317), and hatred may be concealed by apparently good relations. German Jews loved German culture, Hankin observes, yet 'There was no closeness between the two peoples, it was one-sided love, the proximity between Jews and German is false' (p.61).

One of the most grotesque explorations of the Holocaust is carried out by Sam, who suggests that Lionel use in the poems he writes,

> twenty-one thousand curtains of the Ark of the Law. Seventeen tons of brown and black hair, six tons of blond hair, two tons of gold and silver teeth, eight million pairs of shoes, one million six hundred thousand pairs of earrings, two million three hundred thousand silver candlesticks, two million spice-towers [used at the conclusion of the Sabbath] made of silver and other metals. Two tons of diamonds, thousands of kilometres of train journeys, coal for trains, rail repairs, engagement of rail workers, thousands of kilometres of barbed wire and coils, thousands of tons of gas, bullets, spades for burials, crematoria, one million five hundred thousand used beds, factories, shops, research institutions, fur hats, cork hats, felt, material, wool. Crowns for teeth, phosphate from bones, fat for soap, suitable cooking ovens, cars! Money, dollars, marks, zlotys, francs – altogether more than three billion dollars, machines, printing presses, socks, overcoats, carpets, works of art, decorative objects, and more. (p.312)

For Kaniuk the Holocaust should not be 'used' in this or any other way, but he acknowledges that it cannot be depicted at all without doing so to some extent. He implicates himself in his account of how Ebenezer appears, together with Shmuel, in a nightclub performance called 'The Last Jew', which provides the title for the book and its central image. Their performance consists of reciting the Jewish collective memory learnt in the camp, for Ebenezer believes that with the death of each Jew this knowledge dies, involving each surviving individual in the struggle to preserve it (p.252). Some characters, however, are regarded as having a more entrepreneurial relationship with the Holocaust, one that provides them with a living and even a certain reputation: for example, the sculptor Tamarin (doubtless an allusion to the famous sculptor, Tamarkin) specializes in expensive Holocaust memorials (p.322).[50] The Holocaust theme is closely associated with the loss of life that occurred during Israel's various wars and which preoccupies Hankin's group in particular, and indeed, he is the bridge in this novel between these historical events.

Testimony becomes self-defeating once it is industrialized and commercialized.[51] The details of Boaz's memorial-business activities, including all expenses, salaries and income, are reported with grotesque accuracy in a lawyer's report to the revenue office. In this it is explained how,

> between the years 1952 and 1972 the company paid full salaries to 46 sculptors and 200 workmen (carpenters, tinsmiths, ironmongers, decorators, speakers, cantors, the burial society, embroiders of flags, painters, graphic designers, drivers, investigators, interviewers, tape operators, maintenance workers and more). The company employed an adviser from the Bergen Belsen Society for two years with a full salary and there were royalties on printed material – all adding up to one hundred thousand dollars. The cost of a Holocaust memorial is not possible to mention here. (p.322)

However, Boaz's ambitions can be guessed at by the regret he expresses at not having been given the opportunity to erect a fifteen-storey memorial on the hills near Castel 'with a revolving restaurant on top, reading rooms, memorial rooms and pictures of every victim of Israel's wars, thousands of pictures identical in size, with more rooms for future ones, memorial rooms for the victims of the Holocaust and for the ghetto fighters. Guides in uniform will explain the wars and salvation' (p.463). Noga is the one who notes that when 'the death of strangers becomes a "business" in the ordinary sense it becomes monstrous' (p.333), turning the human desire for commiseration into a financial transaction (pp.334, 336). Boaz macabrely 'builds scenery for the dead' (p.336), but the grotesqueness of his work is revealed when he (or possibly Sam) proposes to young soldiers on the eve of battle that they write a poem, including their full name, address and army number, for their families to treasure should they be killed (pp.468–9). Kaniuk carefully describes a similar grotesque industry developed by Melissa's father to commemorate her life (p.464).

Alongside the formal memorializing of events, loss of memory and individual and collective memories all play an important part in the book. Ebenezer has 'no personal memory' (p.78) but acts as a kind of vessel for remembering, recording everything he says and hears 'in order to remember' (p.255) even things 'there was no need to know, and that no one could or should know by heart' (p.82). As the Last Jew, he is custodian of 'the memory of all generations' (p.81). His medical report (pp.248–57), which suggests he lacks a self, likens him to the character in Robert Musil's book, *The Man Without Qualities* (originally published 1930–42; English translation 1953–60), a non-human (p.255), a historical document based on facts alone. Ebenezer, in the role of the Last Jew, has no power of judgement, and it is only when we, as readers, integrate collective with personal memory that we activate this power. Kaniuk's references to Musil's work, in which Musil presents his philosophical view of an existence oscillating between the worlds of reason and mysticism, point to Kaniuk's belief that fiction alone can encompass all aspects of modern life. The figure of the Last Jew, which haunts the novel – promising, although no one knows when, to become a reality (p.470) – is temporarily Ebenezer, the keeper of Jewish memory (p.82), until he begins to recover his own memory, which he realizes 'is a sign that I am not the last Jew ... a sign that I also begin to remember things that happen to me' (p.180). Preserving memory means that there is someone for whom to preserve it.[52]

In an interview, Kaniuk explained how the words 'the Last Jew' and the role of this figure in his novel are based partly on a former neighbour, a carpenter who alone of his family had survived Auschwitz and who, having listened to Kaniuk's description of a writer's work in progress, said to him: 'writing cannot bring back my daughters'.[53] The failure of the writer to do more than witness and preserve history helps explain why the novel 'is structured from the end to the beginning' (p.27, also p.399), lacking a chronological sequence, time flowing from future to past.[54] For Kaniuk, Jewish time runs from the end to the beginning (p.399), 'a prophecy forward and backward, like the history which is slowly vanishing from the face of the earth and only historians are left without history' (p.463). A thousand years pass back and forth (p.470), interspersed with temporal landmarks such as Ahad Ha-Am's visit to Palestine (p.153), the pre-war departure of Jews from the country (p.145), the end of Baron de Rothschild's administration, the Balfour Declaration, the arrival of the first British Consul (p.212) and of Holocaust survivors to fight in the war of Independence (pp.21, 106). Ebenezer recites Kavidius's ancient story on the one hand, as well as a book published in 1984, entitled *The Sources of Moses's Burial*, describing Sinai and the monastery of Santa Catherina long before Israelis were allowed to travel there. Hankin thinks this book is described as if in the distant past (p.287), although it is actually recent. The past and the future have no logical sequence.

Kaniuk's fictional world is ruled by a kind of Puppet-master, the surreally named General Manager of the Solar System, living in Berlin, who orchestrates the whole of Jewish history and observes how Jews:

> clung to one thing which has no basis in any reality: words. They had a language before they had houses, they had grammar before they had land; this is why they could create a future even though they had no past ... The land which the Hebrews desired was hard, dominating, capricious, a hater of masters, uncompromising ... The Hebrews had to succumb to their most terrible desires so that they should know better than anyone else how to win in lost wars. This is why they invented defeat as a sign of their life and survival as a code of life. The Hebrews always knew the longings for extremes, which is why they were so stubborn, and with their own hands they created for themselves the tools which always brought disaster upon them. (pp.109–10)

Rivka explains that big dreams inevitably have small endings (p.460), yet 'perhaps we did do something important after all; perhaps this settlement and the whole enterprise are not as small as I think, perhaps there was something in Nehemiah's vision which did not completely evaporate and was not unnecessary' (p.229). Without dreaming, she fulfilled a dream. Kaniuk voices through Rivka his severest criticism of the Zionist enterprise, since she – a widow and critic of Zionism rather than a New Jew of the kind imagined by the early Zionists – is the one who becomes a legend in her own lifetime, although facts about her life have to be altered to fit her legendary status. As Hankin's wife observes, 'the past can be improved through eternity' (p.71). The emptiness of what was achieved, however, is reflected in Rivka's view of nationhood as 'a flag with land' (p.141) or in Boaz's memory of how at school 'we used to sing the national anthem, *Hatikvah*, as if it were a swearing-in ceremony in the name of the Bar Kochba Revolt; even the declension of verbs had a national nuance' (p.48). On Boaz's return from war he meets the nursery-school teacher who had taught him the value of dying for his country and tells her: 'The soldiers died for you, proudly carrying to their grave the lofty words you made them learn by heart. Did it help them? So you have a flag!' (p.266). It is remarkable that as early as 1982, when the novel was first published, Kaniuk seems to predict the collapse of the Zionist enterprise. Yet, his constructive conclusion is that memory is the only way to secure Jewish survival.[55]

This ultimate conclusion distinguishes Kaniuk's thinking from that of such writers as Moshe Shamir, who in *Be'mo Yadav (Pirkey Elik)*[56] outlined the 1948 generation's ideology of dissociating themselves from exilic Jewish existence to create an antithetical 'New Jew'.

Kaniuk's character Nehemiah speaks for those early Zionist opponents of exilic 'degeneracy' (p.129) as well as for their gradual disillusion, because although 'the harder the way, the greater Nehemiah's love of this country became' (p.155), 'Nehemiah's great ideals could not survive fever, typhoid and thieves' (p.150). Kaniuk suggests that the attempted regeneration has failed, and sends Ebenezer, the son of a New Jew, to Europe to reconnect with Jewish history. The impossibility for Ebenezer and, by implication, the Sabra (native-born Israeli Jew) generation of reconnecting with Jewish history is a central concern of the novel, and Kaniuk offers an alternative, at least for some. It is only Noga who grasps this solution and acts on it. Noga falls in love with Boaz and moves in with him (p.333), suffering a miscarriage and attempting suicide (p.282) before becoming pregnant again at the age of 45. It seems highly significant that she refuses to reveal whether the father (p.461) is Sam or Boaz. This uncertainty and disorientation suggests how for Kaniuk the identity of the next generation must result from an integration of what seems to him every aspect of Jewish experience.

Whilst Kaniuk endorses the integration of memory and the Jewish experience, he is critical of what he sees as the Israeli obsession with death and the dead, which is here what links the Holocaust and the War of Independence. The lives of war-bereaved parents, especially Hankin and his wife and the Shimonis, organizers of the bereaved parents' meetings, as well as those of Germanwriter and his wife Renata, are dominated by their dead. Hankin describes how 'I thought in concepts of the grammar of nothingness, the grammar of life, or no-life, and the grammar of the nothingness of my son was suddenly absolute, like declining a verb which has no future and has no past and therefore, perhaps, no present tense' (p.36; see also pp.28–9). But his wife, with whom the narrator's sympathy lies, is unable to express grief through organized activities. She never leaves the house, weeps quietly (p.33), refuses to be comforted by her husband or join the ceremonial visits to their son's grave (p.34) and despises the group's meetings, which are described as a grotesque 'group dance of graves' (p.57). Absurdly, each participant insists their son died a hero (which is known in some cases to be untrue) and some even that rays of light shine from their graves (p.71). The memorial ceremonies in which they participate are interspersed with texts on heroism and self sacrifice from the Bible and writers such as Alterman or Bialik (p.57), and are so melodramatic that Hankin feels ridiculous wearing the clothes he reserves for memorial ceremonies (p.74). But Mrs Shimoni, in whose home the meetings take place, enthusiastically suggests they propose to the Ministry of Education a syllabus on widowhood and bereavement. She explains to participants how 'she spoke about it with a famous psychologist, and the psychologist wrote a research paper about the art of Israeli bereavement, how the "togetherness" of committees such as ours dulls the pain, and perhaps one should teach people before a catastrophe happens to them, and thereby save them the difficult years that we all went through until we found a way to live with the catastrophe' (p.77). Later, in a further criticism of this obsessive behaviour, Noga asks for her name to be removed from the list of volunteers for teaching 'widowhood, bereavement, orphanhood and commemoration' (p.337). Among other characters involved with the dead, Matan Ba-Seter, Yardena and Sam are in love with dead people, Hankin's neglected house is compared to a grave (p.30) and Rivka smuggles her husband to Palestine in a coffin.

It has been noted that 'through the glorification of self-sacrifice for the sake of the nation, the early Jewish settlers created nothing but spiritual death ... Moreover, in their attempt to create a "New Jew" they were guilty of another, more serious falsification. They tended to erase the past completely.'[57] The way in which this drive to forget moulded reactions to the Holocaust and its survivors can be seen in the account of how Hankin, helping to smuggle illegal immigrants ashore in 1939, brings home a pale young man wearing braces and a rotten belt and with yellow teeth. 'I remember how I sat that evening and the boy spoke German because he knew no other language, and he told stories the mind refused to believe. I understood every word but something in me rebelled, I could not speak with him, only mumble' (p.55). Hankin's reaction, which typified that of the Yishuv, leads Kaniuk to conclude that Hankin, 'despite his Sabra persona, has longed all his life for the German-Jewish element in him'.[58] Kaniuk deplores the need to 'create the past according to the needs of the present and live as much as possible in a fictionalized past' (p.262), showing Hankin wishing to believe his son Menahem to have been more than an ordinary young man and at least a poet (p.240), his death to have been justified and for him to have been 'a son worthy of an ideal, so that he could love him' (p.247). Hankin, an educator from the founding generation of the State, wants to raise a generation of New Jews who will 'fight for the souls of their parents and their friends' (p.278), and is prepared to attribute to them 'exaggerated' qualities (p.66). Boaz, unable to tell Hankin the truth concerning Menahem's death, devises a version that makes him into a national hero (pp.244–5), and even invents an account of how his friend had saved his life in the battle for the Old City of Jerusalem (pp.238–9). Immediately after the passage in which this is revealed, which includes realistic descriptions of the fighting, Hankin discovers that Menahem had in fact died pointlessly in a skirmish which never even entered the history books (p.240). It was 'a miserable generation, which tried to become the answer to their parents' dreams, which the parents should instead have killed' (p.330). Menahem's mother, another of Kaniuk's positive female characters, explains how 'I raised a son and knew just who he was. Menahem didn't want the big time. He wanted a nice life, the sea, doing nothing, just living. That's all he wanted. Not very inspiring, maybe, but human' (p.280). Noga, another woman who understands the value of ordinary life and dreams of being married to a man who cycles to work in a bank near home (p.337), confronts her parents' generation with the charge that 'you taught me how to live with death, you did not teach me to live with life. It's become a national characteristic' (p.337), and she imagines children eventually being born with built-in guns (p.352).

So, for Kaniuk the identity of the next generation must result from an integration of every aspect of Jewish experience. In order to achieve this it is necessary to reconnect with Jewish history through the preservation of memory. Kaniuk proposes that the search for identity undertaken by each Jew[59] should encompass not a single homogenous identity, but several, changing over time and fusing with collective memory. But although Bartana suggests that Kaniuk is addressing the multiple Jewish identities available in modern Jewish history, including secular and religious ones, the novel considers only secular options. A single character in the novel, a labourer wearing a skullcap, believes not in redemption through Marx and Engels, but 'prays ... patiently for the Messiah' (p.218). Yosef Reina accuses Nehemiah and his friends of trying to kill God (p.130) and wonders if Hibbat Zion ('the Lovers of Zion' movement) would blow away the dust of centuries from the pages of the Bible (p.133). The founders of the State are secular Hasidim (p.343) who arrive in Eretz Israel full of ideology, but build a country of shopkeepers, turning redemption into a new ghetto (p.344). Ebenezer's father-in-law, Mr Klumin, believes in the need for 'a Hebrew monarchy like that of Rome, with a senate and an enlightened king'. Zionism is for him not only a solution to the troubles of the Jews – or their return to their homeland – but an act of historical justice' (p.225). Hankin is Kaniuk's mouthpiece for expressing disappointment with the results of efforts 'to conquer ... land for the nation' (p.38). 'All his life he did the same things, loved one woman, one son, one home, one country, one language, one dream ... and suddenly – the rationale which no rationale recognizes' (p.47).

Kaniuk confirmed in an interview that the dichotomy between Israeli and Jew, central to the thinking of the founders of the State, seems invalid to him. Indeed, 'it is at this conjunction between Jew and Israeli that, unlike my generation, I have a deep sense of being a Jew. I am from Tel Aviv, but also from over there.'[60] Boaz and Shmuel/Sam, the twinned Sabra and Holocaust-survivor, each incomplete without the other, represent Jewry for Kaniuk. Ebenezer, a Sabra who fights in the 1948 war, is merged with Shmuel, the concentration-camp survivor, who has a number tattooed on his arm (p.78) to symbolize their shared fate and the skills by which they survived, Ebenezer by woodcarving and Shmuel by 'burying and burning corpses and trading with the golden teeth or diamonds hidden in the rectum' (p.103), including that of his father (p.193). Ebenezer recognizes that a New Jew such as his son Boaz would not have survived the Holocaust without Shmuel's skills (p.379). Their fusion, for Kaniuk, produces the identity that will emerge among the children and grandchildren of the founders of the State.

NOTES

1. Yoram Kaniuk, *The Last Jew* (Tel Aviv: Hakibbutz Hame'uchad, 1982). All translations are my own. *The Last Jew*, brilliantly translated by Barbara Harshav, is published by Grove Press, New York, 2006.
2. Stuart Hall and Paul du Gay (eds), *Questions of Cultural Identity* (London: Sage Publications, 1996), p.4.
3. Amela Einat's reply to S. Sheffer, *Iton 77* 6, 32–3 (1982), p.71.
4. Avraham Hagorni, 'There is Method in the Madness', *'Al Ha-Mishmar*, 14 May 1982, p.7.
5. Yoram Kaniuk interviewed by Ruth Keren, *Moznayim* 69, vol.6 (March 1995), p.17.
6. Gabriel Moked, 'Human Condition as a Conceptual Scenery', *Ha'Aretz*, 18 June 1982, p.16.
7. In an interview 'Like Someone Who Arrived from Another Place', published in *Mikan*, Keter, Volume 3, (Dec. 2002), Kaniuk said, 'I feel deep closeness to Jews anywhere in the world, and less to Israelis' (p.184) ... 'I wanted to write about a man who is in fact two: born in Europe, a Holocaust refugee, and who is also an Israeli' (p.188).
8. Ortsion Bartana, 'The Anatomy of Jewish Melancholy', *Yediot Ahronot*, 12 March 1982.
9. Esther Hanoch, 'Agnon's Tradition and Modernism of the 1960s: A.B. Yehoshua, Yitzhak Orpaz and Yoram Kaniuk' (unpublished PhD dissertation, Tel Aviv University, 12 June 1986), pp.65–8.
10. Hagorni, 'There is Method in the Madness', p.7.
11. Amnon Navot, 'Yoram Kaniuk, The Last Jew', *Ma'ariv*, 4 June 1982, p.37.
12. Giora Leshem discusses the difficulty of deciphering *The Last Jew*. See his article 'The Last Jew', *Prosa* 58–9 (1982), pp.21–2.
13. For the medieval story of Kavidius, in which Jewish–Christian relations are represented as based on guilt and the desire for murder, see Gershon Shaked, *Hasiporet Ha'Ivrit, 1880–1980* [Hebrew Narrative Fiction, 1880–1980] (Tel Aviv: Hakibbutz Hameuchad and Keter, 1998), Vol.5, p.182.
14. See also pp.210, 295, 325–7, 349–51, 364, 366–72, 373–6, 384, 407, 410–12, 416, 422, 434–43, 458, 464.
15. Yoram Kaniuk interviewed by Ruth Keren, *Moznayim*, p.19.
16. Literally 'A gift in secret [pacifieth anger]', *Proverbs* 21:14.
17. In a recent conversation with Yoram Kaniuk, he mentioned to me that he had always been fascinated by messianism and over the years has spent a great deal of time studying this historical phenomenon.
18. For more on Joseph Della Reina and his function in the novel see Yael Poyas, 'Myth in *The Last Jew* by Yoram Kaniuk' (unpublished MA dissertation, Department of Hebrew and Comparative Literature, University of Haifa, March 1991), p.50. Yoram Kaniuk, *Aunt Shlomtsion the Queen* (Tel Aviv: Hakibbutz Hameuchad, 1976); and idem, *The Death of a Donkey* (Ramat Gan: Sifryiat Makor, 1973).
19. The same can be said of Sam's absurd visit to Melissa's parents (p.309).

20. For example, pp.73, 86, 107, 111, 118.
21. Hasya to Renata (for example, pp.240, 279), Hankin to Germanwriter (for example, p.283).
22. As is emphasized in bold type on p.243.
23. For example, pp.208–9, 444.
24. See, for example, pp.307, 312, 319, 362.
25. For more on this device called *'mise en abyme'* see Naomi Hanas, *Faces Reflected in the Mirror; The Narrator as a Writer in the Self-Conscious Literature in the Hebrew Novel from Brenner to Grossman* (Tel Aviv: Hakibbutz Hameuchad, 2003), p.200.
26. Yoram Kaniuk interviewed by Ruth Keren, *Moznayim*, p.16.
27. Gershon Shaked, 'Through Many Small Windows, by the Back Door: An Introduction to Postrealistic Hebrew Literature, 1950–80', *Prooftexts* 16 (1996), p.279.
28. On the use of myth see Poyas, 'Myth in *The Last Jew* by Yoram Kaniuk', especially pp.6–36.
29. See also pp.175, 177, 178.
30. As in pp.230, 259, 260, 269, 270, 281, 282, 286, 287, 302, 319, 341, 357, 367, 408, 410, 432, 447, 455, 469.
31. As in pp.10, 20, 24, 46, 58, 59, 65, 75, 83, 84, 85, 90, 91, 92, 118, 126, 127, 133, 134, 147, 171, 174, 177, 185, 283, 294, 296, 297, 298, 300, 301, 302, 309, 312, 316, 318, 328, 329, 330, 348, 354, 369, 374, 384, 396, 398, 399, 403, 404.
32. Poyas, 'Myth in *The Last Jew* by Yoram Kaniuk', pp.112–14.
33. Yoram Kaniuk, *Adam the Son of a Dog* (Tel Aviv: Amikam, 1969). Hillel Barzel, in *Mesaprim Be-yichudam* [The Best in Hebrew Prose: Essays on Modern Hebrew Novelists] (Yahdav, 1981), pp.237–9, points out similarities between Kaniuk's *The Last Jew* and Kafka's *The Trial*, including the image of the dog, which recurs in Kaniuk's *Wasserman* (Tel Aviv: Hakibbutz Hameuchad, 1988).
34. For example, pp.88, 259, 269, 270, 285, 286, 289, 307, 313, 358, 396, 427.
35. Shaked, *Hasiporet Ha'Ivrit, 1880–1980*, Vol.5, p.191.
36. Ibid., p.193.
37. Nurit Goertz, *Motion Fiction: Israeli Fiction in Film* (Tel Aviv: Open University of Israel, 1993), p.272.
38. Shaked, *Hasiporet Ha'Ivrit, 1880–1980*, p.183.
39. See S. Sheffer, 'The Last Jew, A Different Direction', *Iton 77* 6, 32–3 (1982), p.70.
40. Navot, 'Yoram Kaniuk, The Last Jew', p.36, stresses the importance of reading *The Last Jew* in the context of Kaniuk's earlier works. A vulture has previously appeared, as has Shlomtsion the Queen, here Rivka Schneersohn.
41. See Poyas, 'Myth in *The Last Jew* by Yoram Kaniuk'. Nilly Flumin particularly emphasizes the mythologizing of women in Kaniuk's writing.
42. Moked, 'Human Condition as a Conceptual Scenery'.
43. Israel Barama, 'History as Consciousness in *The Last Jew*', *Moznayim* (Feb.–March 1983), p.49.
44. Hanoch, 'Agnon's Tradition and Modernism of the 1960s', p.89, and Barama, 'History as Consciousness in *The Last Jew*', p.50.
45. See also pp.30, 74.
46. Esther Hanoch's extensive work does not address this absence from the novel of the Oriental community.
47. On Merar see pp.147, 155, 181, 212, 237, 260, 266, 319, 338, 339, 386, 462, 467, 470.
48. Kaniuk interview with Risa Domb, 17 July 2001.
49. Ibid.
50. For further examples see pp.463 and 464.
51. Barama, 'History as Consciousness in *The Last Jew*', p.51.
52. Ibid., p.50.
53. Kaniuk interview with Risa Domb, 17 July 2001.
54. See Hanoch, 'Agnon's Tradition and Modernism of the 1960s'.
55. Interestingly, 'the poetics of memory' (as Shaked termed it in *Hasiporet Ha'Ivrit*, Vol.5, p.130), is the guiding principle in David Shahar's works, where the present can be understood only in the context of the past.
56. Moshe Shamir, *Be'mo Yadav (Pirkey Elik)* [With His Own Hands (Chapters on Elik)] (Tel Aviv: Sifriyat Poalim, 1952).
57. Ruth Spira, 'A Fictional Past', *The Jerusalem Post*, 9 April 1982.
58. Shaked, *Hasiporet Ha'Ivrit, 1880–1980*, pp.285–6.
59. Hanoch, 'Agnon's Tradition and Modernism of the 1960s', p.280.
60. N. Beretzki in an interview with Kaniuk, *Ma'ariv*, 7 Feb. 1986.

5

The Poetics of Unsaying: The Identity Crisis of the Modern Jew in *The Story of a Life* by Aharon Appelfeld

Aharon Appelfeld's painful search for the childhood roots he lost during the Holocaust, and his struggle to forge for himself an identity in his newly adopted homeland, found expression in, among other works, *The Story of a Life*.[1] This is a fascinating book for what it shows about the role of memory in the construction of private and collective identity, and the nature of the identity being sought.

Appelfeld was born in Czernowitz in 1932 to assimilated parents who 'saw themselves as an inseparable part of European intelligentsia' (p.153). His mother's parents, whom he loved deeply, were orthodox Jews living as farmers in a small village away from the big city. One uncle was a rich, secular and enlightened landowner who nevertheless, unlike Appelfeld's parents, continued praying and studying Talmud. When life began to be difficult for Jews just before the outbreak of the Second World War, his father, a successful industrialist, tried to extract the family from Europe but failed to do so. Appelfeld survived a ghetto and a labour camp, losing first his mother and then his father, and managing at the age of 10 to escape into the forest on his own, hiding his Jewish identity and somehow surviving the war. He recalls living in the house of a prostitute, serving her in exchange for a meagre lonely existence until she threw him out. However, Appelfeld himself rejects the notion that he should be labelled as a 'Holocaust writer' so that part of his life is not dealt with here.

Recent years have seen an unprecedented explosion in the writing of biographies, autobiographies and memoirs both in Israel and elsewhere. One of the reasons for this literary phenomenon is the blur in the postmodern era between factual and fictional narration. The traditional distinctions between biography, autobiography, personal history (diary/confession) and novel are starting to be questioned. Since biography and autobiography serve as catalysts in the shaping of personal and collective identities, for many contemporary writers, Appelfeld included, autobiography is not merely a device for summing up the accumulated wisdom of a lifetime, but a means of defining identity.

Writing about lives is an ancient practice. Biographies have been important in the form of genealogical, religious and didactic texts since the start of recorded literature. Autobiography as such, including diaries and personal letters, began to appear in the sixteenth century and became widespread in Europe by the eighteenth century. Autobiographical writing includes autobiography and memoirs, two distinct modes of writing, although they are often thought interchangeable. Memoirs customarily give some prominence to personalities and actions other than the writer's own; some are accounts of historical events that have been directly witnessed by those recording them. Autobiography, on the other hand, is a connected narrative of the author's life, stressing introspection and the significance of one's life against a wider background. It is artistically shaped and coherent. However, not all biographical works fall into these classifications. In an attempt to reflect this, the term 'life writing' has gained wide academic acceptance since the 1980s, both because of its openness and inclusiveness across the genre, and because it encompasses the writing of one's own or another's life as well as memoirs.

Autobiography and biography were alien to traditional Jewish Hebrew culture because of the secondary status given to the individual in Judaism. There are relatively few autobiographies in classical Hebrew and medieval Jewish writing, and the arrival of autobiographical writing during the Haskalah period can be seen, as Alan Mintz pointed out, as an aberration in the development of Hebrew literature.[2] The collapse of religious cultural hegemony at the turn of the twentieth century prompted the creation of autobiographies, some of which crossed over into fiction, such as in the works of the writers Mordecai Ze'ev Feierberg (*Whither?*, 1899), and Joseph Hayyim Brenner (as, for example, *In The Winter*, 1903), who developed the genre of fictional autobiography in Hebrew writing. They described the crisis of the personal life of the 'uprooted' young Jews (the *Tlushim*) who broke away from religion, family and community, and their unsuccessful attempts to live in a world empty of those beliefs and institutions. Although these works are not strictly speaking autobiographies, they reflect the individual's ordeal, which was considered significant because it was representative of a collective crisis. With the events of the First World War and the Russian Revolution and their traumatic effect on Jewish life, the focus in Hebrew autobiography shifted from the author to the events themselves, as in Avigdor Hameiri's *The Great Madness* (1929).[3]

This trend continued when the cultural centre of the Jews moved finally in the 1920s from Europe to Palestine. The new settlers were engaged in rebuilding their national homeland. This is probably the main reason why Zionist leaders in particular wrote autobiographies. Autobiographies were deemed acceptable since they seemed to be part of the Zionist national enterprise, in which public events took precedence over the private life of the individual. In the fictional autobiographies that appeared in Hebrew after 1948, the names of the narrators may not be those of the authors, but the people and events are authentic and the documentary and historical data accurate. Like the Haskalah writers, those of the 'Generation of the State' portrayed through the individual the life of a generation in crisis. The collective, rather than the individual, is central, and themes concerning the War of Independence and commitment to the newly established Israel and its ideology were paramount.

In the 1960s, writers of the so-called New Wave Generation brought marginalized individuals into the limelight, and consequently many writers of the preceding 'Generation of the State' have recently turned to writing documentary-style autobiographies, in which they themselves are the protagonists, albeit under assumed names. These narratives contain extracts from journals, letters and memoirs, all of which reinforce the concrete and historical elements and undermine the fictional aspects of these works. Examples of such works, which include autobiographical descriptions of the writer's youth in Europe or in Israel, are Matti Megged's *A Borrowed Name* (1985); Nathan Shaham's *Sealed Scrolls* (1988); S. Yizhar's *Mikdamot* (1992), *Tsalhavim* (1993), *Asides* (1996) and *By the Sea* (1996); and Nurit Zarhi's *Games of Loneliness* (1998).[4] Significantly, Haim Be'er's *The Pure Element of Time* (1998) marks a departure, since his autobiography reveals his intimate life and uses his real name.[5] Works such as Yoram Kaniuk's *Post Mortem* (1992), Natan Zach's *Death of My Mother* (1997) and Amos Oz's *A Tale of Love and Darkness* (2002) contribute to this new development.[6] This is the context of Appelfeld's *The*

Story of a Life. However, whereas in the works mentioned above the use of unmasked autobiographical details departs dramatically from the authors' previous fictional writings, this is not quite the case for Appelfeld. In some ways, all of Appelfeld's work can be regarded as 'life writing', since his fictional narratives contain autobiographical elements that are not difficult to detect as such and which have become merely more transparent in this work. We can trace these elements more easily here than in his other writings, possibly because they all allude specifically to the Holocaust, an event inherent in the shaping of Appelfeld's life as well as in his poetics. Although *The Story of a Life* presents fragmented chapters of Appelfeld's life, and despite the author's insistence that it should be regarded neither as autobiography nor as a chronological narration of life, but as chapters of memory and observation[7] or as an 'inner tale' (p.8), nevertheless *The Story of a Life* can be considered to be 'life writing'.

Memory is one of the most significant elements of life writing, its preservation being an important component of identity. Appelfeld struggled to gain an identity by linking his past and his present through memory. In the modern world, individual memories acquire significance as the guarantors of social continuity. 'Memory is by nature multiple and yet specific; collective, plural, and yet individual'. The French historian Pierre Nora suggests that 'through "identity", the singularity and permanence of the self (or group) are asserted; in "memory", the repertoire of representations of an individual or collective past is embraced as the distinctive repository and resource of a present consciousness.'[8] Seen in this way, the preservation of memory has an important function and, as Michal Goldvicht noted, the 'pains of memory of the Diaspora, of being a refugee, and of assimilation, secretly nurtures the here and now'.[9] In The *Story of a Life* Appelfeld strives to make sense of the chaos of life in general and of his own personal experience in particular. He presents different chapters and episodes in an attempt to reach the roots of his life and to reconnect with them (p.8). The trauma of his experience of the Holocaust required his memories to be banished to 'the inner cellars of the soul' (p.7). A great deal has been written about the prevailing Zionist ideology, which insisted on the suppression of survivors' memories,[10] but Appelfeld also examines the personal, self-imposed suppression of memory. It seems that only while serving in the army did his suppressed memories surface and lead him to his past, to the world in which he grew up and to which he felt connected (p.128). It is worth noting that Appelfeld's memories of the war years are of a specific kind: they are memories of a child, not an adult. Not surprising then, that he describes them as if they are imprinted in the cells of his body and as instinctive sensations rather than as clear images (p.83) or explicit, specific memories. Smell, damp shoes or a sudden noise can take him back into himself. 'I do not invent, I draw from the inner depths of my body sensations and thoughts that I absorbed during my blindness' (p.169, also p.49). Thus, Appelfeld claims that it was his senses that informed him of his experience, not words, and insists that words are false, that they 'cannot confront big catastrophes' (p.96). Undoubtedly this is the source of his Poetics of Silence.

Theodor Adorno, the German sociologist and philosopher, famously argued, that, 'After Auschwitz, to write a poem is barbaric ... It means to squeeze aesthetic pleasure out of artistic representation of the naked bodily pain of those who have been knocked down by rifle butts ... Through aesthetic principles or stylization ... the unimaginable ordeal still appears as if it had some ulterior purpose. It is transfigured and stripped of some of its horror, and with this, injustice is already done to the victims.' This is an issue that preoccupies several of the writers discussed in this book, especially Shaham, p.29, and Kaniuk, pp.47–9. Adorno expressed the traditional aesthetic idea that the representation of a horrible event, especially if in drawing upon literary skills it achieves a certain graphic power, could serve to domesticate it, rendering it familiar and in some sense even tolerable, and thereby shearing away part of the horror. The use of literary forms is likely to soften the impact of what is being rendered, and in most rendering of imaginary situations we expect and welcome this phenomenon. But with a historical event such as the Holocaust – an event regarding which the phrase 'such as' cannot be employed – the chastening aspects of literary mimesis can be felt to be misleading, a questionable way of reconciling us with the irreconcilable. The question arising from this argument is whether there is a human form of language adequate to the conceptualization and understanding of Auschwitz, or whether the limits of language fall short of the limits of the Holocaust experience itself? The question of the limits of representation is, of course, not new. There is always a dichotomy between historical and fictional truth. But, the disjunction between language or form, and subject matter such as the Holocaust, creates a moral dilemma. To this dilemma there are two diametrically opposed reactions: on the one hand, given the absence of usable norms through which to grasp the meaning of the scientific extermination of millions, given the intolerable gap between the aesthetic conventions and the loathsome realities of the Holocaust, writers of the post-Holocaust era might be wise to be silent; silent, at least, about the Holocaust. This was the Jewish German poet Paul

Celan's view. He believed that words make plain sense, and therefore by trying to represent the Holocaust the writer becomes a collaborator. His life's work was to unsay. (Ironically, Paul Celan was 'unsaying' through the medium of his poetry.) On the other hand, other writers, such as Primo Levi, saw it as their duty to say. Levi argued that there couldn't be too much documentation about this most extreme of human experience. The problem for him was how to say it, not whether to say it. Appelfeld deals in his book with these moral and aesthetic dilemmas. The poetics of his writing is the poetics of 'unsaying', the poetics of silence. He acknowledges the fact that he cannot find words to describe his Holocaust experience itself. He cannot touch 'that fire', he can only tell of something else that is somehow related to it.

A similar view of the role of words and silence in literary texts is expressed by the Holocaust survivor in Anne Michaels' book *Fugitive Pieces*: 'I listened to these dark shapes as if they were black spaces in music, a musician learning the silences of a piece. I felt this was my truth. That my life could not be sorted in any language but only in silence.'[11] Appelfeld needed to rediscover the silence of the war years and to revive it so that he could find himself. But with what words and in what way? These are the very same questions that Primo Levi had asked. Not surprisingly, when Appelfeld tried to describe the story of the forest, where as a 10-year-old child he was forced to hide, all words 'evaporated' (p.164), seeming banal and unable to convey the experience itself. Yet it is paradoxically through words that Appelfeld sought his rehabilitation and searched for the reconstruction of memory and the self.

In the process of reconstruction of the self, the 'acquisition of the new language was the greatest challenge'.[12] When Appelfeld arrived in Palestine in 1946 at the age of 14 he found he had no language at all. 'What can I do with no language?' (p.102), he asked. This handicap affected his whole existence. The Hebrew language, exotic though it sounded, was difficult for him to pronounce (p.100). The loss of his mother tongue represented the loss of his home, his parents and the world to which he had belonged. After the lonely war years, the long and formative period of time during which he had hardly used words (p.111) and had had to work hard on learning to pronounce them (p.49), he found it difficult to communicate, was hard of speech and became capable of narrating with the utmost brevity (p.113). In order to overcome his stuttering he read German and Hebrew and memorised whole sentences so that he could learn how to speak again. Between 1946 and 1950, while working in the fields of the agricultural college at Nahalal in the Jezreel Valley, Appelfeld struggled to learn Hebrew, the Bible and Bialik's poetry (p.101). The Zionist written and unwritten slogan for new immigrants at the time was: 'Forget, integrate, speak Hebrew, improve your appearance, and nurture your manliness' (p.126). Whoever spoke in his mother tongue was sternly rebuked, and he hated those who forced him to speak Hebrew (p.101). Appelfeld's mother tongue died away, and at the age of 18 he could not write properly in any language. He finally wrote in a language that he had initially resisted. One of the first steps to integration in a new society is adopting the native language. However, Appelfeld recalls that it sounded to him like a language of soldiers imposed on him by force. Hebrew was a stepmother to him (p.103). This reaction resembles that of Kafka, a writer whose style influenced Appelfeld. Kafka, a Czech writing in German, created a language that, like Appelfeld's, was distinguished by its economy and by the fact that its syntax was different from the dominant German of Prague. Both writers de-territorialized the language, to use Gilles Deleuze and Felix Guattari's terminology.[13] A recent study reveals that a similar process can be detected in the poetry of Yehuda Amichai, Nathan Zach and Dan Pagis.[14] Perhaps this is the reason why Appelfeld is seen as, in the linguistic sense, in exile. As Sidra Ezrahi pointed out, for Appelfeld 'the Hebrew language seems to provide neither a bridge nor a window onto the past'.[15] There is no doubt that the role of the Hebrew language is an all-encompassing issue in the debate of the identity of the Jewish people, their roots, their religion and the way forward in every aspect of their being. For many, their language is inseparable from their identity.[16] (For more on this in relation to the Oriental writer Sami Michael, see pp.67–77.)

Appelfeld experienced the sense of not belonging, and forever asked himself: 'Who am I and what am I in this country?' (p.125). He felt he belonged neither 'here' nor 'there'. Survivors were forced to dissociate themselves not only from their mother tongue, but altogether from the world of their past, to forget it and to integrate into what was for them an artificial world (p.154). They had to become Jewish farmers and fighters, were criticized when they failed to do so, and had to defend themselves from unfair attacks. While he envied survivors who were able to forget and to integrate, he could not do so. He could not submerge himself and assimilate into a Palestinian/Israeli existence (p.138), perhaps because he refused to obliterate his past in order to build a new life on its ruins.[17] As mentioned earlier, memory was central in his struggle to shape or reshape his own self. He strove to connect his new life to his childhood, which might have contributed to his decision to become a writer, since he was afraid that the story of his childhood and of his parents and grandparents might be lost forever (p.165). The world of S. Yizhar and Moshe Shamir, the popular writers of the 1950s in Israel, was not his world, however. Their total commitment to idealism was alien to him and stood in stark contrast to his earlier life and experiences (p.105). Their negation of the Diaspora led them to disconnect from the long history of Jewish life in Europe. Yigal Schwartz pointed out that Appelfeld is closer to older Hebrew and Yiddish writers who represented the *shtetl* (a small Central or East European town or village with a large Jewish population) than to Israeli writers.[18] They were connected to Jewish life in Europe, to the world Appelfeld had lost. Dror Burstein draws interesting parallels between Appelfeld and the painter Yossel Bergner, and suggests that because both view Israeli reality through the lenses of the ruins of the European world, both are regarded as exilic, alien and non-Israeli artists who do not belong and who represent a world that has died.[19] This seems misguided. That part of the European world which has died is an inherent part of Israel and both artists do represent Israeli experience. The effects of the Holocaust on all aspects of Israeli life, the increased ethnic awareness and the new phenomenon of the 'born-again' Jew has brought about a Judaisation of secular society. Having previously identified themselves as Israelis, many writers have become Israeli Jews, and that is often reflected in the representation of their characters.

Appelfeld became a writer for refugees, rather than for ideological Zionists. This was not an easy path to choose, as the reading public in the 1950s and early 1960s, when Appelfeld began to publish, was receptive to survivors' memoirs and authentic testimonies, but not to fiction representing the Holocaust experience. Appelfeld, as an immigrant, a refugee, a person who carries inside him the child of the war, explains, 'fiction was regarded as provocation' (p.97, also p.141). However, most of the teachers at the Hebrew University who influenced him when he first started to write, such as Dov Sadan, Martin Buber and Gershom Scholem, were born abroad and like him, carry the pain of two homelands. From them he learnt that a homeland is not necessarily a geographical locus, but can be transported (p.138). He came to the conclusion that 'here' and 'there' are not as disconnected as Zionist slogans insisted, and in this respect Appelfeld stands apart from mainstream Israeli writers. He was attracted to Yiddish and Hasidic literature, both of them antithetical to the emerging Israeli culture, but it was precisely through Yiddish literature, even though it was looked down on, that Appelfeld hoped to rediscover his ancestors in the Carpathian Mountains and through it to reconstruct his identity.

In the 'New Life' club, established in Jerusalem in 1950 for survivors from Galicia and Bukovina, he found a surrogate home (p.166). There he heard familiar languages such as Yiddish, Polish, Russian, German and Romanian, and saw faces that reminded him of his lost life. His whole writing enterprise can be seen as a journey back home, in other words to Europe. Perhaps this contributed to the frequent claim, or even accusation, that he is a 'Jew writing in Hebrew in Israel rather than a typically Israeli writer'.[20] 'Typically Israeli writer' he is clearly not, but an Israeli writer he is. Appelfeld has always been aware of the distinction between these two identities and, as Gershon Shaked noted, he 'writes for the Jews of Israel, reminding them that, perhaps against their wishes, they are not only new Hebrews but also old Jews'.[21]

Appelfeld focuses again and again on one problem: the identity crisis of the modern Jew.[22] In *The Story of a Life* he testifies to his search for authentic Judaism, showing sympathy towards traditional Judaism which he terms 'post-assimilatory'.[23] Unlike in his earlier days, Appelfeld no longer stands apart from the concerns of the mainstream. Zionist ideology and Israeli identity are in a state of disorientation not least because this is typical of modernity and results from the openness and pluralization of social life, as well as of increased choices.[24] Amid a puzzling diversity of options and possibilities, one of the more attractive choices for Israelis seems to be the reconciliation between early Zionism and Judaism.[25] Secular Israelis today may reopen their old 'Jewish Bookcase' and draw from it new meanings. 'Jewish' and 'Israeli' no longer seem antithetical, and this ongoing reconciliation will no doubt lead to new options. Appelfeld reached that conclusion long ago, for in his life writing, the need to preserve memory, and to link the past with the present, guided him in shaping his own identity.

NOTES

1. Aharon Appelfeld, *Sippur Hayim* [The Story of a Life] (Jerusalem: Keter, 1999).
2. Alan Mintz, *Banished from Their Fathers' Tables: Loss of Faith and Hebrew Autobiography* (Bloomington, IN: Indiana University Press, 1989); and Risa Domb, *Encyclopedia of Life Writing*, ed. Margaretta Jolly (London and Chicago: Fitzroy Dearborn Publishers, 2002), pp.477–9.
3. Avigdor Hameiri, *Hashigaon Hagadol* [The Great Madness] (Jerusalem and Tel Aviv: Mizpeh, 1929).
4. Matti Megged, *Mem* [A Borrowed Name] (Tel Aviv: Sifriyat Poalim, 1985); Nathan Shaham, *Sefer Hatum* [Sealed Scrolls] (Sifriyat Poalim, 1988); S. Yizhar, *Mikdamot* (Tel Aviv: Zmora Bitan, 1992); idem, *Tsalhavim* (Tel Aviv: Zmora Bitan, 1993); idem, *Tsdadiyim* [Asides] (Tel Aviv: Zmora Bitan, 1996); idem, *Etsel ha-yam* [By the Sea] (Tel Aviv: Zmora Bitan, 1996); and Nurit Zarhi, *Mishakei Bedidut* [Games of Loneliness] (Israel: Yediot Ahronot, 1998).
5. Haim Be'er, *Havalim* [The Pure Element of Time] (Tel Aviv: Am Oved, 1998).
6. Yoram Kaniuk, *Post Mortem* (Tel Aviv: Ahronot, Chemed, 1992), Natan Zach, *Mot Eemee* [Death of My Mother] (Tel Aviv: Hakibbutz Hameuchad, 1997); and Amos Oz, *Sippur 'al Ahava Ve-Choshech* [A Tale of Love and Darkness] (Jerusalem: Keter, 2002).

7. It seems to me, therefore, that Shaked's accusation of omissions and selectivity in Appelfeld's life is not justified. See G. Shaked, 'Haberiha Meha-metsioot', *Ha-Aretz* [Escape from Reality], 20 April 1999.
8. Pierre Nora, 'Between Memory and History: *Les Lieux de Memoire*', in *Representations* 25 (Winter 1989), p.9.
9. Michal Goldvicht, *Ha-Aretz*, 21 Feb. 2002.
10. On the indoctrination of Zionist ideology with reference to Appelfeld's work, see Yigal Schwartz, *Individual Lament and Tribal Eternity, Aharon Appelfeld: The Picture of His World* (Jerusalem: Keter, 1996), pp.45–6; Sidra Ezrahi, 'Revisioning the Past: The Changing Legacy of the Holocaust in Hebrew Literature', *Salmagundi* (Fall–Winter 1985–6), pp.245–70; Alan Mintz, *Hurban: Responses to Catastrophe in Hebrew Literature* (New York: Columbia University Press, 1984), pp.203–39. See also Hannan Hever, *Producing the Modern Canon: Nation Building and Minority Discourse* (New York: New York University Press, 2002), especially the Introduction, pp.1–10.
11. Anne Michaels, *Fugitive Pieces* (London: Bloomsbury, 1996).
12. Gila Ramras-Rauch, *Aharon Appelfeld, The Holocaust and Beyond* (Bloomington, IN: Indiana University Press, 1994), p.14.
13. See the article by Gilles Deleuze and Felix Guattari, 'What is a Minor Literature', in *Mikan*, Ben-Gurion University of the Negev (May 2000), pp.134–43.
14. Nilly Sharf-Gold, '"A Boat Carrying Longings": The Big Journey in the Sea and its Imprints in the Poetry of Amichai', in *Mikan*, Ben-Gurion University of the Negev (Dec. 2002), pp.86–100.
15. Sidra D. Ezrahi, *By Words Alone* (Chicago: Chicago University Press, 1982), p.370.
16. Y. Bronowski expressed concern regarding the loss of the homogony of the Hebrew language as an important component of Israeli identity as a result of the recent Russian immigration in Israel. See 'Marak Hatarboot Shel Akeret Habayit' [The Housewife's Soup of Culture], *Ha-Aretz*, 10 April 1998, p.13b.
17. For an interesting comparison between Y. Bergner's painting and Appelfeld's prose in the presentation of the destroyed world of their European childhood see Dror Burstein, 'Mikarov', *Yediot Ahronot*, No.7 (Winter 2001), pp.86–101.
18. Yigal Schwartz, *Individual Lament and Tribal Eternity, Aharon Appelfeld*, pp.83–4.
19. Dror Burstein noted that both Bergner and Appelfeld depict the Jewish European world on the eve of its destruction. Both artists paint it as a perfect, self-contained world which resembles a coloured bubble, unaware how thin its skin is.
20. Gershon Shaked, *Sifroot'az Kaan ve-achshav* [Literature Then, Here and Now] (Tel Aviv: Zmora Bitan, 1993), p.143. Also many critics mentioned in Schwartz, *Individual Lament and Tribal Eternity, Aharon Appelfeld*, p.195.
21. Gershon Shaked, 'Appelfeld and His Times: Transformations of Ahashveros, The Eternal Wandering Jew', *Hebrew Studies*, University of Wisconsin-Madison, xxxvi (1995), p.100.
22. Schwartz, *Individual Lament and Tribal Eternity, Aharon Appelfeld*, p.111.
23. In his article in *Ha-Aretz* ('Haberiha Meha-metsioot'), Shaked is unfairly critical of this post-assimilatory attitude, claiming that Appelfeld's escape from Israeliness to his European past brings him closer to radical Diaspora assimilated Jews than to those who claim to have an Israeli identity.
24. For further discussion on the subject see A. Giddens, *Modernity and Self-Identity* (London: Polity Press, 1991), pp.1–9.
25. A.B. Yehoshua, *Hakir ve-hahar* [The Wall and the Mountain] (Tel Aviv: Zmora Bitan, 1989), p.56.

6

The Loneliness of the Wanderers: *Water Touching Water*[1] by Sami Michael

Studies of Hebrew literary works rarely mention the role of Oriental Jews in the construction of the new Israeli identity. Indeed, significantly, all the authors discussed in this book so far are of Ashkenazi (German or East European) origin, while the Oriental origin of the subject of chapter 7, A.B. Yehoshua, was not expressed in his earlier works and not often in his later ones[2]). This is because the voice of the Oriental, or Sephardi, was hardly heard in the literature of the early stages of Statehood. Prior to the arrival of the Jews from Arab countries the Sephardi community was a very small minority in Israel, even though a hundred years or so earlier they had been the decisive factor in the choice of the accent of the Hebrew language adopted by the newcomers from Europe (see pp.13–14). The mass immigration of Jews from Arab countries, particularly from Iraq (more than 120,000 immigrants), occurred between 1948 and 1951, after the establishment of the State of Israel, and therefore their impact could only be felt and expressed in literature written subsequently, but even then their voices were not much heard until the 1970s.[3]

It is outside the scope of this study to analyse the reasons for this late arrival, but a contributing factor was no doubt the fact that the Jews arriving from Arab countries were initially considered culturally inferior to the European Jews and aspects of their culture were therefore not incorporated into the structure of the identity of the New Jew, which was conceived in Europe. It was not any lack of ability to incorporate an ethnic culture into the new Israeli identity that prevented it from being considered, but rather a rejection of that component in favour of a European one. It was a conscious, well considered decision. In addition, it seems that the early Oriental writers downplayed the Jewish dimensions and Jewish communal life: 'The religious aspect of the characters' Jewish identity is of such little significance as to be nearly irrelevant. The primary identification as Jews is imposed on these characters from the outside.'[4] This might have added to the marginalization of the Oriental culture during the earlier stages of Statehood as it did not fit with the Zionist vision of the new identity for the New Jew, a Jew who could be free in the ancestral homeland for the first time in over two thousand years of exile, and who would negate the characteristics associated with the exilic Jew (for more on this, see pp.63–4). Thus, the creation of the so-called New Jew was inevitably bound up with creating a new identity for the Jews which would not be defined by religion alone.

The immigrants, who arrived in the Homeland from all corners of the world, brought with them their own different cultural identities. The Zionist movement sought to melt these down in the melting pot of the new State and to unify all into one single homogenous identity that would be strong enough to withstand the multitude of obstacles on the way to a national revival. A.B. Yehoshua supported this strategy: 'I think that this step was correct. It was correct to suppress, correct to pour a new concrete floor for a new identity. I think that the Orientals who took this step benefited from it. It was healthy for them and healthy for culture.'[5] In hindsight, this policy may have been too harsh for the incoming immigrants, who were forced to abandon their cultural background and adopt a new identity, in keeping with the Zionist belief that this was the fastest and most effective way to succeed in the struggle for national survival.

Indeed, this approach was bemoaned by Dror Mishani in his review of Sasson Somech's autobiographical book: 'As I was sitting in a coffee house writing this review, it was as if this typical street of Tel Aviv suddenly doubled, and as if behind it you could see the coffee houses of Al-Rashid Street. It suddenly became clear to me how richer Israel could have been with the help of Baghdad, yesterday as well as today.'[6] In her work *Exile from Exile – Israeli Writers from Iraq*, Nancy Berg confirms this superior attitude of the European Jews and says that:

> In addition to being uprooted from home and living in unfamiliar, harsh conditions, the Iraqi Jew suffered an immediate fall in status partially arising from the difference in cultures (different values and priorities) and partially from a prejudice on the part of the new society, which

assumed that Jews from Arab countries were less modern and less educated. A professional or a businessman who had been highly respected in Baghdad would be asked if he was familiar with electricity and plumbing, and if lucky, would get a job as a day labourer. Physical work, disdained by the elite in Iraq, was glorified in the pioneering culture of the newly established State of Israel.[7]

Even though the same fate befell many of the highly cultured immigrants coming from Germany for example (the *'yekes'*), their cultural background was not generally looked down upon. It has been suggested that the Oriental cultural background was deliberately presented by writers such as Sami Michael, Shimon Balas and Eli Amir 'as a test to the liberalism of Israeli culture and to its ability to enable the presence of ethnic culture'.[8]

Sami Michael's book describes one such immigrant who is struggling hard to integrate into the new society in Israel, yet who unlike the European immigrants, strives to preserve his own cultural background and to reconcile the new identity with the old.[9] Even though it is in many ways a flawed work, it has much that is of relevance to the questions of identity under discussion here.[10]

Yosef, the protagonist, arrives in Israel from Baghdad in the early 1950s. The autobiographical elements are overt. Sami Michael arrived in Israel in 1949 at the age of 26. At the Brenner Prize 2004 ceremony, Sasson Somech, another important Baghdadi writer, observed that the recipient Sami Michael[11] wrote about social and ethnic problems, Arab–Israeli relations, and issues of war and peace but above all in all his novels he incorporated autobiographical details.[12] This was significant, given the rarity of fictionalized autobiographical writing before 1948. What autobiographies were being written were generally by public figures and focussed on their careers; few discussed the authors' personal lives. There was a brief flurry of fictional autobiography at the turn of the century from such writers as Ze'ev Feierberg and Y.H. Brenner, but after the First World War the focus largely shifted to memoirs about the Zionist enterprise and the Jewish settlement. It was only after 1948 that writers turned again to fictional autobiography, when the portrayal of the collective rather than the individual was central, and the dominant themes were the war of independence, and commitment to the newly established Israel and its ideology.[13] (For more on this, see pp.58–60.)

Water Touching Water is the moving story of an immigrant, who could also be any displaced person. But the fact that this particular immigrant is a Jew arriving from an Arab country is of particular interest here. The story takes place during the 1950s, soon after the establishment of the State of Israel and during the period when food is still rationed. It tells of Yosef, who is in his twenties and a newly arrived immigrant from Baghdad, who has come to Israel not because of his Zionist belief, but who, like Sami Michael himself, was obliged to escape Iraq because he belonged to the Communist party. Yosef had spent most of his youth in Baghdad in the underground. When he arrives in Israel he feels as if 'someone has taken a saw and cut his life into two. One part remained in Baghdad and one part is here' (p.26). The country that has offered him refuge demands him 'to die as an Iraqi to be born again as an Israeli' (p.286). This was a painful demand, and until more recently (with the rare exceptions of writers such as Appelfeld, see pp.62–4, and Agnon), one which was not often expressed by the European immigrants, who were ideologically committed to the Zionist enterprise and as such sought to put their past behind them. Indeed, Yosef accuses the Israelis of lack of sympathy. 'You are offended when I say that I am longing for the street where I grew up. You do not understand how one can long for something which is not Israeli' (p.26). In his interview with Dalya Karpal, Sami Michael explains: 'I grew up in an Arab country, my mother tongue was Arabic, and after a few hours flight I found myself in Israel with a different identity.'[14] Thus, the cultural wealth of Jews from Arab and Islamic countries was suppressed and therefore could not contribute to the making of the new identity.

Yosef is further alienated from his previous existence by virtue of his political commitment to communism, which cannot be accommodated by Zionism. He is therefore not offered a suitable job by the Employment Bureau (p.55) and is compelled to work as a clerk for a Baghdadi lawyer and rent a room in Haifa from an Arab woman in an Arab neighbourhood. Sami Michael himself lived in the same Arab neighbourhood (Wadi Nisnas) when he first arrived in Israel, and like his protagonist he too was lonely, away from his family and friends. Yosef, just like Sami Michael, leaves behind the young woman to whom he is betrothed, not believing that as a Jew she can ever escape from Iraq. He 'bore in his heart the horrendous emptiness of a man who was uprooted from his home' (p.36) and is aware that after three years in Israel he behaves like an alien in his country and even among his own people. (Sami Michael himself testified that he wanted to belong to Israel, but 'The Arabs look at him like an Israeli Zionist, and the Israelis look at me as someone who came from there – with heritage and language and manners of the enemy.'[15]) Yosef admits that he would probably have felt and behaved similarly had he found himself in the Argentine or Turkey. 'He was still not a ripe citizen in Israel' (p.273).

The fact that he uses the term 'still' suggests that he is hoping that he will eventually be able to integrate. But initially Yosef lacks confidence in his new homeland, and 'ever since the day he arrived in Israel he always tried to avoid sitting in a vacant chair before making sure that it did not belong to someone' (p.14).

However, it is worth noting that Yosef's experiences in his new homeland are presented subjectively, entirely from his point of view; the reader thus has no opportunity to actually witness the Israelis' reactions to him, and this one-sidedness seems to be a flaw in the narrative. By contrast, his Hungarian friend Nemet, the Holocaust survivor, feels that 'humanity and history owe him' (p.14).[16] He therefore behaves unapologetically, and ironically, as a result, integrates better. Sami Michael compares the difference between the Ashkenazi and Sephardi reaction to Israel. However, the contrast is by no means so clear-cut or universal – on many occasions elsewhere he has pointed out that the superior attitude of the Israelis to the Holocaust survivors was no less degrading than the attitude to the Oriental newcomers. Another character in the novel, a Baghdadi wedding photographer, also suffers from the superiority of the European Jews. He wants to change his name from Abdallah Abu Kar'a to an Israeli sounding name so that he can get more work from Ashkenazi clients. Ironically, he chooses an Eastern European sounding name, Grisha Rosenberg, asking 'what can be more Hebrew than that in Israel?' (p.44). Thus for the Oriental immigrant the terms 'Israeli' and 'Ashkenazi' are one and the same.

The theme of the Sephardi ethnic inferiority (which is not as overt here as in Sami Michael's previous books[17]), is relevant to the examination of the process of the evolving identity of the new society in Israel. The author argues that in some respects there are in fact many similarities between the Ashkenazi and Iraqi Jews. His protagonist, Yosef, believes that the differences generally cited between the two ethnic communities are unfounded. When Ya'acov asks critically why it is that the Jews of Baghdad did not escape Iraq in time, Yosef answers: 'And when did European Jewry leave its home and emigrate to Israel? Only after Hitler destroyed their home. Were it not for the pogroms in Eastern Europe and for Hitler, it is doubtful if there would have been an echo to the Zionist message' (p.57). It seems that this historical equation is somewhat distorted. Although Zionism was undoubtedly accelerated by the Holocaust, it was a firm national force beforehand. Presumably, Sami Michael is using this argument to suggest that the superiority held by the European Ashkenazi community is unjustified and unfair. Another case for this argument is made when his father-in-law Ya'acov boasts that his wife Hannah's family has been in the country for over ten generations. Yosef's reply is that his family can boast a hundred: 'This is how long, if not more, my family has been in Iraq. We have been there since the destruction of the First Temple' (p.112). He feels that this should be considered as respectable a lineage as any other. There should be no preference for the Zionist lineage. Why should Yosef, who is an Oriental immigrant, be inferior to Ya'acov and Hannah who belong to the founding fathers of the State, the 'salt of the earth' (p.177)? True, he acknowledges that their generation dug wells and built houses in the new land, and 'nearly always under fire' (p.195), but should this make them superior? Yosef points out that the Iraqi Jews are just as industrious as the Israelis. 'Believe me, we were more strict then you in matters of being industrious. At the age of twelve laughter and playfulness were regarded as despicable qualities. A man who developed a hobby which did not have practical benefit was considered to be frivolous' (p.202). Yosef also argues that his earlier commitment to Communism was no different to the commitment of the Zionists. 'He belonged to a serious generation who carried the redemption of the world on his shoulders, a generation who saw itself the last for "shi'abood" [enslavement] and the first for redemption, enrolled to the demanding ideals of the collective' (p.294). Yosef challenges Ya'acov, the New Jew, by asking: why is one better than the other? As history has shown, unfortunately this argument has not been resolved by Zionism, which sought to create one homogenous society, sharing one dominant ideology.

When the novel opens, two lonely immigrants, Yosef and Nemet (who has recently left his wife having discovered that she is having an affair with another man), meet two young girls on Shavey Tsion beach near Nahariyah. The relationship between the two girls and Yosef is central to the story. Ktina, as indicated by her name (*katan* means 'small'), is a tiny, good-looking 22-year-old; by contrast, her friend Smadar is a tall, striking, red-head. Smadar, who is already married and seemingly pregnant, arranges for Yosef and Ktina to meet again and a relationship develops between the two. Ina, Ktina's nickname, is strange, obsessively afraid of darkness and obviously hiding some unstable emotional state. Surprisingly, after a short courtship, Ina and Yosef get married (p.63) against the better judgement of her parents, Ya'acov and Hannah. They do not attend the wedding, but despite their objections, continue to spoil and protect their only daughter, giving the couple a fully furnished villa by the sea, very near their own home.[18] Because of his parents-in-law's opposition, Yosef is not happy to become a beneficiary of their wealth. However, he treats his wife gently and patiently while he struggles to understand her apparent psychological problems. He does not find out about Ina's mental illness until she mysteriously disappears one day, never to be found again. Only then does Ya'acov tell him of the army officer who had assaulted and tortured Ina in her army camp, and of the attempted suicide that led to a total mental breakdown. Using his high-ranking position, Ya'acov had arranged for the officer to be sent to America under a false passport, but he returned to Israel and continued to terrify Ina and eventually abduct and murder her. Finally, he hangs himself, thereby preventing Ya'acov from taking his revenge. Only now is the secret of her pregnancy disclosed to Ya'acov. This tragedy brings Ya'acov and Yosef together, and a deep friendship and dependency develops between them. As Sasson Somech pointed out, the names Ya'acov and Yosef allude to the biblical father and son and suggest the nature of their relationship.[19] It seems that their ideological differences fell apart in the face of the tragedy and for the first time the two men were able to face each other as equals, 'as a man is facing a man, a sorrow facing sorrow'.[20] It was a 'friendship of emptiness' (p.306), but a touching one. Heartbroken, Ya'acov and Yosef move in together. Ya'acov's wife Hannah, a historian of the Byzantine period in Palestine, remains in the marital home, though she spends every afternoon and evening with them, cooking and managing the household, and the couple treat Yosef like a son.

Ya'acov and Hannah Golan belong to the first generation of the State, to the elite who established it. Ya'acov had been a very high-ranking officer in the Israeli secret service and possesses the qualities of a leader (p.41). However, Yosef is critical of some aspects of the values held by the model of the New Jew. He asks a very pertinent question, which has preoccupied Israeli society in recent years and which is at the centre of this study: 'Ya'acov Golan is an Israeli through and through. How much Judaism was preserved in him?' (p.54) Yosef, like some of the European characters in the texts analysed earlier in this book, demands that we should not forget that first and foremost we are Jews (p.61). But, the question that Sami Michael is not able to answer is: what identity should these Jews have? Yosef is critical of the secular option offered by Zionism, accusing Ya'acov of adopting the wrong values and priorities: 'You worship hills and earth. You look at a fighter plane decorated with blue and white and tears of a grandparent drip from your eyes. Is this Judaism? And you speak of exilic Jews as if they were unclean animals' (p.61). Sami Michael offers an alternative to the Zionist option: an Israeli identity which excludes Zionism! 'I am an Israeli patriot, but I am not Zionist ... Being a Jew is deeper in me than being an Israeli'.[21] But what does being a Jew consist of? In his interview with Dalya Karpal he argues that his Judaism manifests itself in the feeling of solidarity that he shares with other fellow Jews wherever they are and whatever language they speak. This solidarity is above and beyond their ideologies or their national belonging. But what does this 'solidarity' mean? Religious? Cultural? Ethnic? National? The sociologist Yehuda Shenhav, also of Oriental origin, quotes his grandmother, who mourned that 'Israel destroyed the (Jewish) people'.[22] But, this is a harsh judgement. Indeed, Israel sought to change but absolutely not to erode the identity of the Jew. The formulation of an identity is not a static process and it is to Israel's great credit that the search and the debate are still going on.

Yosef cannot identify with Ya'acov, who represents the founding members of the State, and who belongs to a generation that despises weakness (p.250) and raises their children on pride and determination, claiming that without them 'we could not exist in this country' (p.273). Ya'acov does not hesitate to offer up the best children and to send them to their death in the battles for national survival (p.274). For him, the army serves as the dividing wall between life and death, and creating a myth of heroism has become a necessary product for self preservation. Sami Michael has suggested elsewhere that Zionism created a secular culture that has only a thin layer which is likely to crumble. Although he is an Israeli Jew now, his antecedents, going back 2,500 years, lived amongst gentiles. Yosef is also critical of the Israeli attitude to the Arabs. He is sympathetic to them and criticises the Israeli authorities, whose 'barking' diggers 'bite the deserted Arab houses to prepare the ground for governmental offices' (p.45). Whereas for his Ashkenazi friend Eli Philosoph, 'every Arab that he did not know personally was an enemy' (p.181), Yosef has to admit that in Baghdad 'Arabs saved him more than once from Arabs. There were some who even sacrificed their life for me' (p.186). However, this issue is beyond the scope of this study.

It is Smadar, Ina's best friend, who organizes a job for Yosef with the Water Authority where she works, and from then on she becomes more and more significant in his life. Eventually she discloses her love for Yosef when he is recovering in hospital from a serious accident at work, and their love culminates in Smadar giving birth to their son, although she is still married to her husband and has had a child by him as well.

Alongside his job, Yosef is writing a first novel in secret, but the transition from Arabic to Hebrew is hard for him and he finds it difficult to describe a reality in a language which is foreign to it (p.39). This is a problem for all writers who are torn away from their natural mother tongue, a theme also explored by Aharon Appelfeld (see pp.62–3). For a while Sami Michael (like Yosef), was writing in Arabic while living in Israel. He observed that similarly, the late writings of the Yiddish writer Scholem Aleichem deteriorated when he moved from Poland to America. These are self-referential comments which surely reflect Sami Michael's own literary difficulties. The Hebrew lines of the first pages of Yosef's first novel are 'interspersed with words in English and even more in Arabic, a tough testimony to his helplessness in his continued effort to overcome the new language' (p.214).[23] He comes from a culture where prose is still in its infancy and despite the fact that some of his writing is embarrassingly immature, he loves the 'elation which accompanied the miracle of the birth of words on empty pages' (p.234).

The title of the book, *Water Touching Water* (in English: *Water Kissing Water*), evokes the story of the Creation, and to highlight further the element of water, one of Natan Zach's poems is quoted below it on the title page: 'What forced me to be so attracted/ to that to which the heart is attracted/ what forced me to try to separate/ between water and water.' In the final chapter of the novel the protagonist concludes that, 'The waters above and below the earth are those that carry the particles of the crumbling body to wherever it is necessary' (p.395). The book is divided into four chapters entitled First, Second, Third and Fourth Wave. Furthermore, every chapter is divided into thirty-seven shorter sections, each bearing a title combining the word 'water' with some adjectival term which vaguely alludes to the given content. The opening scene, always significant in a novel, takes place on the beach of Shavey Tsion by Nahariya where the vegetation, the sand and the sea not only set the atmosphere of the story but add a metaphorical dimension. Indeed, water appears throughout the text[24] in both literal and metaphorical ways. Furthermore, the protagonist is working for the Israeli water ministry and there are detailed descriptions of the different activities associated with the measuring of water levels in the northern part of Israel, particularly in the hydrometric station on the Jordan in the Hula valley. The excessively detailed descriptions of the work reflect Sami Michael's experience in this field, as for twenty-five years he himself worked for the Israeli Water Authority in Northern Israel.[25]

The water of the title may refer to the Euphrates touching the waters of the Jordan, thus expressing the 'cross breed', or the 'sawed' life of Yosef (and all those in his situation). Sasson Somech suggests that the waters represent the Israeli hydrologist on the one hand and the secret service Baghdadi man on the other, as 'both are "water", namely not typical representatives of a specific human society'.[26] It has been suggested that water is a source of life, the flow of life.[27] But inherently 'water' also suggests isolation, self-containment and possibly in this case, with its continual ebb and flow, its ability to be forever changing and yet somehow always the same, an allusion to its powers of change within constancy, evoking perhaps the situation of the Jewish people.

Yosef's work with water is physically dangerous because of frequent flooding, it is often too near the Syrian border, and under threatening weather conditions in a wild landscape. But, what seems to be of particular significance is that both realistically and metaphorically, the work is always carried out in isolation. Apart from Ina and his close co-worker Eli Philosoph, also a new immigrant, Yosef has little contact with anything or anyone outside his work. 'It was as if the two of them were detached completely from Israel. Under alien sky the loneliness of the wanderers closed up on them' (p.95). This situation diverts the pain of integration into a new, unfamiliar, society and avoids confronting the challenges of having to adopt a new identity.

NOTES

1. Sami Michael, *Water Touching Water*, in English *Water Kissing Water* (Tel Aviv: Am Oved Publishers, 2001).
2. For more on this see Risa Domb, *Home Thoughts from Abroad* (London and Portland, OR: Vallentine Mitchell, 1995), pp.36–61.
3. Probably from the 1960s on. See, for example, Simon Balas, *In The Transit Camp* (Tel Aviv: Am Oved, 1964).
4. Nancy Berg, *Exile from Exile: Israeli Writers from Iraq* (New York: State University of New York Press, 1996), p.148.
5. As quoted by Yitshak Laor in 'The Majority of the Oriental Israelis live somewhat as aliens, or in a pocket of the East', *Ha-Aretz*, 25 March 2005
6. Dror Mishani, 'Memory of someone else is also my own memory', *Ha-Aretz/Sfarim* 4, 25 Feb. 2004; Sasson Somech, *Baghdad Yesterday* (Tel Aviv: Hakibbutz Hameuchad, 2004).
7. Berg, *Exile from Exile*, p.70.
8. Yohai Oppenheimer, 'My Gentle Conqueror', in *Ha'Aretz/Sfarim* 4, 9 Feb. 2005.
9. Ella Shohat termed the Jews from Islamic countries 'cross breeds' in her book *Israeli Cinema East/West and the Politics of Representation* (Austin: University of Texas Press, 1989).
10. In 'The Paradox in the Heart of Being', *Ha-Aretz*, 12 Oct. 2001, p.14B, Sasson Somech suggests that in this novel there is a 'tendency to get away from the psychological-realistic representation and more impressionistic ... Yosef is not a "round" character and we know very little about his family and his past.' Although there are lengthy realistic descriptions, particularly in relation to the hydraulic work of the protagonist and the endless dialogues, there are passages in which there are unacceptable exaggerations verging on parody, such as the description of people queuing up to give information about Ina's disappearance (p.237), or the unlikely wedding party (p.63) and the life-threatening storm on the way to Tsfat (pp.272, 275, 278). The overall effect of mixing these genres is to reduce the sense of authenticity. Further, Michael uses the technique of switching between an omniscient and a first-person narrator, which often interrupts the flow of the story (for example, pp.107–9, 269–90. Chapter 30 tells of the love of Yosef and Smadar; chapter 31 continues with the description of Yosef's accident, when he locks himself in the hydraulic station; chapter 32 continues with Smadar and Yosef, and so on.
11. Sasson Somech, 'Multi Thematic Writer', in *Moznayim* (n.d.), pp.9–10.
12. His novels so far are: *Shavim Veshavim Yoter* [Equal and More Equal] (Tel Aviv: Am Oved, 1974); *Hasoot* [Refuge] (Tel Aviv: Am Oved, 1977); *Hofen Shel Arafel* [A Handful of Fog] (Tel Aviv: Am Oved, 1979); *Hatsotsra Bavadi* [Trumpet in the Wadi] (Tel Aviv: Am Oved

1987); *Victoria* (Tel Aviv: Am Oved, 1993).
13. See Risa Domb, 'Israeli and Modern Hebrew Life Writing', in Margaretta Jolly (ed.), *Encyclopedia of Life Writing* (London and Chicago: Fitzroy Dearborn Publishers, 2002).
14 This and some other autobiographical information is extracted from an interview with Dalya Karpal, 'A Writer Under Influence', *Moosaf Ha-Aretz*, 15 April 2005, pp.24–32.
15. Ibid.
16. Sami Michael's first friends in Israel were from Budapest, and Nemet is based on a real character. See interview with Dalya Karpal.
17. See in particular *Victoria*.
18. Incidentally, the two elderly twin aunts who were the only family members who did attend the wedding, and who expressed their disgust at Ina's choice of an Oriental husband, were in their youth both in love with an Arab (see p.65). Interestingly, this is a reversal of Hanna in Amos Oz's novel *My Michael*, who fell in love with Arab twin brothers.
19. Somech, 'Multi Thematic Writer'.
20. Ruth Livnit, 'Man facing man, sorrow facing sorrow', *Iton 77*, 262 (December 2001), p.6.
21. Karpal, 'A Writer Under Influence'.
22. Yehuda Shenhav, *The Arab-Jews, Nationalism, Religion and Ethnicity* (Tel Aviv: Am Oved, 2000), p.211.
23. For more on the problems of writers, particularly of Oriental descent, adopting a new language for their writing see Berg, *Exile from Exile*, Chapter Four (pp.43–66).
24. See random examples on pp.120, 183, and many more.
25. Karpal, 'A Writer Under Influence'.
26. Somech, 'Multi Thematic Writer', p.10.
27. Kobi Nissim, 'A Lesson in Self Irony', in *Ha-Aretz/Sfarim*, 7 Nov. 2001, p.6.

7

Crossing Borders: The Clash of Civilizations in *The Liberating Bride*[1] by A.B. Yehoshua

Civilization is a cultural entity and is defined by common elements such as language, history, religion, customs and institutions. Language is, of course, central to culture, and literary texts are the very basis of the formulation of identity. However, as Samuel Huntington suggests in his book *The Clash of Civilizations and the Remaking of World Order*:

> everyone has multiple identities which may compete with or reinforce each other: kinship, occupational, cultural, institutional, territorial, educational, partisan, ideological, and others. Identifications along one dimension may clash with those along a different dimension ... The increased extent to which people throughout the world differentiate themselves along cultural lines means that conflicts between cultural groups are increasingly important; civilizations are the broadest cultural entities; hence conflicts between groups from different civilizations become central to global politics.[2]

Yehoshua acknowledges the importance of civilizations to global politics in general and to the Arab/Israeli conflict in particular. He supports Huntington's hypothesis that 'the fundamental source of conflict in this new world will not be primarily ideological or primarily economic. The great divisions among humankind and the dominating source of conflict will be cultural. Nations states will remain the most powerful actors in world affairs, but the principal conflicts of global politics will occur between nations and groups of different civilizations.'[3] Huntington seems to be claiming that differences do not necessarily mean conflict, and conflict does not necessarily mean violence. He goes on to argue that 'the interactions among people of different civilizations enhance the civilization-consciousness of people that, in turn, invigorates differences and animosities stretching or thought to stretch back into history'.[4]

Yehoshua recognizes that there is no universal civilization, but a world of different civilizations, each of which has to learn to coexist with the others. Whilst admitting in an interview held in 2004 that the Israelis have to separate themselves from the Palestinians, believing that 'that's what will guarantee our continued presence here in a hundred years from now',[5] at the same time he warns that they must accept that the Palestinian civilization is different and should be accommodated and tolerated. The efforts of Israel to promote its values of democracy and liberalism, for example, as universal values engender countering responses from the Arab/Palestinian civilization (as suggested in *The Arab in Hebrew Prose* published as early as 1982).[6] No civilization could or should impose its own values on another civilization. It is for this reason that Yehoshua calls for an understanding of the cultural roots of the Palestinians as the key to peaceful co-existence. This seems to correspond to Huntington's theory that 'civilizations unite and divide humankind. The forces making for clashes between civilizations can be contained only if they are recognised.'[7] However, this seems to be rather a naive viewpoint, attractive though it is: whereas civilizations are without doubt important, they do not control states. In the modern era states control civilizations and therefore political clashes are more profound.

The story of *The Liberating Bride*, whose sixth chapter 'The Dybbuk' (pp.377–440) has as its predominant theme the clash of civilizations, takes place in Israel in 1998. It seems interesting to note that when Yehoshua started writing this chapter in 2000, the second *intifada* had just started. Up to that point in the novel Yehoshua expressed optimism and hope for friendly relations between the Israelis and Palestinians. Though the *intifada* shattered his hopes, he did not change the novel, and this might explain certain ambiguities and inconsistencies in the attitude to the conflict.[8] Another interesting point is that the English title is not 'liberating' but 'liberated', one active subject, one passive object. In fact, Yehoshua changed his original Hebrew title from 'liberated' to 'liberating', indicating the double, yet opposite, function of the bride in the novel.[9] The bride assumes both a literal and a metaphorical dimension, and can be seen as representing

Israeli and Palestinian identities, both of which need to be freed from their provincialism and given wings.

The novel tells the story of Professor Yohanan Rivlin,[10] a middle-aged academic, an Orientalist from Haifa University whose progress with two parallel investigations has all but stalled.[11] On the professional level, he is struggling with his historical research into Algeria's war of Independence, unable to find out why the Algerian Revolution after the liberation from French colonialism turned out to be so murderous. On the personal level, he has hit a brick wall in his attempts to discover the reason for his eldest son's divorce after only one year of apparently happy marriage. He is obsessive in his pursuit of answers to these two questions.

In an attempt to inspire him to continue with his work, Rivlin's old teacher and academic mentor, Professor Tedeschi, offers him important research material, left unfinished by one of his most brilliant students who had been murdered by the Palestinians. Rivlin asks Samaher, his young female Palestinian student, to translate the Arabic texts for him.[12] Because of Samaher's obscure illness he is compelled to visit her at home in one of the Arab villages in the Galilee, which he had visited once before for her wedding. The visit to the Israeli Arab village is described by Yehoshua in surreal terms, as are the subsequent visits with Samaher's cousin Rashid, over the border to the West Bank and later to Ramallah. Interestingly, whereas the young Arab boy in Yehoshua's earlier novel *The Lover*, published in 1977, is placed in a realistic situation in a Jewish home in Haifa, it seems that in the year 2001, when *The Liberating Bride* was published, placing an Israeli in a Palestinian or an Arab-Israeli home could only be perceived in surreal terms. Rivlin's search for the secret of his son's divorce leads him to equally surreal situations.

Samaher's cousin Rashid accompanies Rivlin, his wife Hagit and Tedeschi's wife, Hannah, to Ramallah to a song festival, where in a scene very much at the heart of this book, and much to the protagonists' amazement, they are invited to watch *The Dybbuk*, performed simultaneously in Hebrew and in Arabic. Bilingualism is a good example of cultural co-existence and multiplicity of civilizations. It has been suggested that the use of parallel Hebrew and Arabic texts in the novel is a brave and unconventional attempt by Yehoshua to acknowledge different systems of linguistic identities which fix cultural and national identity.[13] However, the long texts in Arabic transliterated into Hebrew, interesting though they are in themselves, ironically have an alienating effect.

The Dybbuk is performed at the festival in Ramallah. This choice is absurd, as indeed is testified by A.B. Yehoshua:

> I wanted to introduce the surreal dimension into life, not to create an alienating absurd, but to find something extra in reality. Take for example the performance of *The Dybbuk* in *The Liberating Bride* in Ramallah. It could certainly be an ordinary and real scene of a meeting of poets. But suddenly I managed to pull out a new thread, which is authentic ... but at the same time it touches on something else.[14]

The festival is meant to celebrate the official opening of the Khalil es-Sakakini Cultural Center in Ramallah, but, perhaps not coincidentally, is postponed to a date that coincides with the fiftieth anniversary of the UN resolution to partition the land. It aims not to be political, but to attract peace lovers, competing with songs of love and friendship (p.404). 'They wanted the Israelis, whether peaceniks or poetry lovers, to feel at home in their hilly city – which, freed of the cruel yoke of occupation, extended to them a strictly cultural welcome on this chilly but brightly lit winter night' (p.437). The festival's director, Nazim Ibn-Zaydoun, is a world-famous Palestinian poet. He is an aging bachelor, somewhat boyish, a self-imposed exile in principle, who flies among the capitals of the world reading his poetry. He declares that 'No entries on political themes would be accepted, even if cast in such lyric form as a Palestinian lament for a field expropriated by Jews, a Palestinian dirge for an olive tree uprooted by Jews, a Palestinian elegy for the childhood memory of a fragrant orange grove built on by Jews, or a Palestinian threnody for the tears of an abandoned horse in a village destroyed by Jews. Likewise, there were to be no refugees, no occupations, no anti-Semitism, no Holocaust, no death, and no bereavement. Only love.'(p.441). However, of course such a demand is not possible to fulfil when people are in conflict, and indeed the poems that are recited are thinly disguised political works. Poetry of the end of the first millennium is read alongside the competition entries (a reference to A.B. Yehoshua's earlier book entitled *A Journey to the End of the Millennium*[15]), which reflects humorously the practical, unsentimental collaboration between Jewish and Muslim desires in the greatest Arab metropolis of the first millennium (p.432), showing the fraternity of Ancient Hebrew and Arabic.

The importance of fictional narratives such as the novel or drama, short stories and even poetry, all of which are incorporated into this novel, seem to be in line with Postmodernist thinking, of equal validity for describing the past as historical documentation.[16] Texts are presented here as a way of understanding the past and possibly reaching reconciliation (or indeed liberation). The past is undoubtedly an important component in the structuring of a collective identity, and

Rivlin's son Ofer is voicing this view when he says: 'After all, unless you know something about the past ... it's hardly possible, and certainly not easy, to make any headway in the present' (p.245). On the personal level, he is hoping that if he and his estranged wife, Galya, can write the two versions of their story they might reach a new understanding (p.251), thereby also perhaps offering a glimmer of hope for the Arab/Israeli situation.

In dealing with the clash of civilizations, the classical play *The Dybbuk* is pivotal to any reading of the novel, and in being performed simultaneously in two languages, the play draws attention to the possibility of multiple interpretations of the same event. As is well known, the Dybbuk is a creature of Jewish legend, a wandering soul that enters a living person's body and talks through their mouth, causing mental illness and creating a separate personality for itself. In 1920 *The Dybbuk*, the play based on the legend and written in Yiddish by S. Anski (Solomon Zeynwil Rapaport), was performed by the Vilna troupe. Interestingly, the play was also called *Between Two Worlds*, evoking the two worlds of the Arabs and the Israelis.[17]

Several characters in the novel seem to be seized by a similar kind of Dybbuk, or irrational obsession. Rivlin is obsessed by his desperate, unsuccessful attempts to discover the secret of his son's divorce. Samaher suffers from mental illness and is admitted to an asylum, possibly obsessed by her forbidden love for her cousin Rashid. She is desperate to be 'liberated' (p.403) from her mental condition and possibly from her arranged marriage.[18] Could it be that her madness is similar to the 'madness' of the bride in *The Dybbuk*, which is mentioned in juxtaposition to her illness? Other obsessions are those of the Lebanese nun who sings at the song festival in ecstasy, as if possessed, and that of Tehila's father and his incestuous relationship with his daughter. These different manifestations of the Dybbuk culminate in the performance of the play in Ramallah. *The Dybbuk's* theme of occupation also has a broader manifestation here, in terms of the inextricable links between Palestinians and Jews occupying the same land and the occupation of 'Arab' land – a topic surely alluded to in some of the love poems recited in this chapter, where two bodies become one, in an uneasy co-existence.

Yehoshua discussed his views on identity, occupation and nationalism in an interview, and explained his idea of extending the concept of Israeli identity to incorporate the Arabs: 'I feel that our nationalism is sufficiently strong, sufficiently stable, it has a land, it has a language and it has a framework of communal life – and therefore it can absorb peoples and identities that previously we thought could not be digested by us.'[19] This idea is analysed in an interesting anthropological study of the novel. Rachel Albeck-Gidron points out that the theme of *The Dybbuk* is based on the idea of cannibalism, which is concerned with the existence of one human being inside another, of one being devoured by the other. The invader is trying to speak instead of the 'host', and the 'host' tries to contain the whole of the 'other' as part of the self. This cannibalistic transgression, alongside the incest transgression, is present in different manifestations in this novel, and it is always in the context of textuality.[20] However, it seems that Yehoshua's protagonist, Rivlin, opposes this idea of the Arabs being an integral part of Israeli identity. Rivlin, who believes in the strategy of unilateral separation between the Israelis and the Palestinians, feels that for the sake of cosmic order the Dybbuk should be separated from the body of the young bride. According to him, this separation is the only alternative to the romantic dream of symbiosis, which is in danger of becoming its opposite, namely turning into arrogant suppressive Orientalism.[21] There seems then to be an unresolved ambiguity between two diametrically opposed possibilities for Jews and Arabs living together. On the one hand, there is the possibility of integration, which contains a forbidden incestuous element, and on the other there is the option of complete separation from one another within fixed boundaries of the self, beyond which there is only the 'other' or the stranger. Yehoshua examines these contradictory desires and wonders if it is ever possible to narrow the distance between them. The desire to cross the borders and to close the gap between the two neighbouring cultures is attractive, but such a symbiosis is conceived in erotic terms, as a dangerous sickness resulting in death or in misery, such as that experienced by Samaher, Rashid and Rivlin.

Yehoshua shows that one way to bridge cultural differences is through the act of translation, particularly of literary texts. Both Hannah Tedeschi and Samaher are translators, engaged in interpretation and identification of myths. The performance of *The Dybbuk* (and in the second chapter of the novel of the biblical text of *Vayomer vayelech*[22]) serves as a model for the role of reinterpretation of myths in structuring cultural identities. Since every translation is an interpretation, the Arabic-speaking audience need some help to understand the 'depth of the Jewish complexity'[23] and ironically need to add to the play a doll-like head of the bride. Through this addition Samaher can be the pursued bride as well as the liberating rabbi who succeeds to drive away the Dybbuk. The dialogue between the Dybbuk and the bride assumes a more personal aspect, as it can also be understood as an indirect yet intimate dialogue between Rashid and his cousin/lover Samaher. They have made of the play a translation of their own situation. The proclamation of the Dybbuk: 'I will not leave this woman. I cannot ... I am joined and conjoined with my mate and will not leave her' (pp.439–40), applies both to Rashid's love and to that of the Palestinians and Jews for their land. After all, the political aspect is present in all the poems even though they are supposed to be about romantic love.

Love is at the heart of this novel – romantic, filial, forbidden – and brides and weddings play a central role. A bride is central in the legend of the Dybbuk, as in the novel as a whole. On the overt level of the text, the bride of the title refers to Galya, the divorced bride of Rivlin's son, Ofer. However, there are other brides in the novel. Samaher is the bride of the opening chapter, 'A Village Wedding'. Another is the bride of the son of the Rivlins' Jewish housekeeper whose wedding opens the chapter 'The Dybbuk'. An analogy between these two brides is inevitable, and through the various props the comparisons – and contrasts – are drawn. Interestingly, perhaps influenced by Vikram Seth's *A Suitable Boy*,[24] Yehoshua decided to open his novel with a wedding. 'I wondered what wedding I can create so that I can enjoy it both as a writer and a reader. And so the idea of an Arab wedding came to mind. And how does one come to an Arab wedding? Via the department at the university, via a female student. So, the combination of Samaher's wedding and of Rivlin's pain for his son's divorce was created.'[25]

As unlike as they are – the Jewish wedding takes place in the autumn whereas the Arab wedding is in the spring; the first wedding is in the Galilee and the second in an industrial estate just outside Haifa – both weddings have a ridiculous aspect. The description of the Jewish wedding is satirical: the bride and bridegroom appear dramatically from behind red velvet curtains like film stars, the bride is dressed theatrically and is beyond recognition. The traditional wedding march accompanies the couple, but is adapted to an Oriental style. There is a film crew and a big screen onto which the ceremony is projected. There is a theatrical aspect to the Arab wedding celebration as well. Both weddings are presented as being ridiculous, but each reflects the different cultural framework within which they belong. Weddings act as cultural constructions of civilizations, or microcosms, and therefore exemplify the societies in which they occur. Rivlin feels equally out of place at both, whereas his wife Hagit is comfortable and popular wherever she goes, suggesting that her own personal humanity is more significant than Rivlin's more academic interest in people and history.

The similarities and differences between the two weddings seem to serve as an indicator for possible fluidity between cultures. Borders are fixed, but one can cross them. In Yehoshua's writings, blurred sight is a repeated leitmotif.[26] In this novel the idea of blurring of borders, metaphorically and literally, is central. There is also the blurring of borders of family relationships. The physical crossing of the border of Israel, towards the 'Palestinian Autonomy' is surreal: 'Gradually the billboards changed from Hebrew to Arabic, and they saw that the border was close. In the end, they flew across it' (p.422). The actual crossing appears undramatic. One side of it is the continuation of the other. It seems that the extensive use of the 'border' metaphorically or otherwise suggests that its rigidity is artificial. Fluidity is inherently natural and indeed desirable.[27] Yehoshua prefers to leave the question of the borders open, like the actual border, which is also not really visible. Fuad, the Israeli Arab from Abu Ghosh, who has worked in Galya's family's hotel for many years, sets clear and definite boundaries between himself and his employers so that their personal difficulties do not impinge on his ability to perform his professional duties. He also exemplifies borders, being an Arab living with, and working for, Jews. He writes poetry but is too ashamed to read his poem at the festival because he feels that 'I have hung around you Jews for so long that my Arabic is like a rusty faucet'(p.443), while Rivlin points out that Fuad's Arabic has become impoverished because of his enslavement to the hotel. Nevertheless, Fuad steps across the border to take part in the festival, just as Samaher steps across one to become a Jew for the performance.

In an interesting interview with Yotam Reuveni in 2003, Yehoshua discusses the idea of lack of borders, or boundaries, as a defining factor in the shaping of Israeli identity. He suggested that Jews find it very easy to inhabit the identity of other peoples. 'We have a formula for it, and this is what we have done throughout our history. We inhabited other peoples' identity without understanding the meaning of it ... We had the sense of lack of boundaries of Jewish identity because it could penetrate (infuse?) anywhere ... Zionism strove to amend this inherent lack of boundaries.'[28] Indeed, the essence of Yehoshua's identity is within very fixed boundaries: the geography and the language. 'I cannot see myself in any other identity.'[29]

Unstable identity can bring about hatred and disaster. Yehoshua believes that one of the ways to avert it is to try and understand the Arabs, 'and if I cannot understand them rationally, then we need to explore and understand them through their poetry'.[30] His protagonist Rivlin is aware of the power of literature. He believes that the magnificent poetry written 1,500 years ago might explain present-day murders and terror (p.105). In the Arabian Peninsula in the seventh century, it was language that provided the unifying element. Poetry forged a common identity, overcoming the fragmentation of all dialects, to provide the basis for homogenous memory.[31] Through the legends and poetry that Samahar translates for Rivlin he strives to reach the truth, to get to know the Algerian people who kill each other. Poetry is the spiritual DNA of people and its history. Similarly, he believes that the Arab secret, its irrationality, can be deciphered through Arabic literature.[32] However, Hagit, the down to earth and practical judge, wonders if Tedeschi, the leading Israeli Orientalist, does not feel that he should sometimes meet real, living Arabs rather than the abstract, theoretical characters which he encounters via his computer screen (p.419). It seems that Tedeschi's investigations are flawed, since literature is after all no substitute for direct contact.[33] It is Hannah, his wife, who dares to step outside the cosy confines of the familiar academic world. Ironically, through her husband's death which occurs at that very same time, just as she is attending the performance of *The Dybbuk*, she is one of the liberated brides in the novel.[34]

Other texts are presented as part of Rivlin's thesis dealing with the Algerian national disaster and by implication comparing it to the Palestinian national disaster. Rivlin suggests that one of the reasons for the confused national identity of the Algerians is their prolonged existence under French rule.[35] Surely Yehoshua is pointing a finger at his fellow Israelis, warning of the dangers of a similar situation with the Palestinians under Israeli rule. It has been suggested elsewhere that despite the historical and geographical differences between French colonialism in Algeria and Israeli settlement in the West Bank and Gaza, there is a strong case for drawing an analogy.[36] Unstable existence leads to confusion and irrationality. What happened to the Arabs in Algeria can be likened to what happened to the Palestinians. The meeting between Europe and Islam after the Algerian Revolution also has parallels with the dialogue between Judaism and Islam. However, it can be seen more specifically in the context of clash of civilizations rather than in terms of conqueror and conquered: 'The current civil war in Algeria is more a war of languages fighting for cultural space than it is a war between religious and secular society' (p.377).

Rivlin's analysis of the political situation and of the source of conflict between Jews and Arabs is seen critically by his colleague, Efraim Akri, an Oriental religious Jew, who expresses a negative view of political settlement in the Middle East. He is critical of Edward Said's famous book *Orientalism*, as well as of the attitude of those Holocaust survivors who believe that their past suffering legitimizes aggression. Another methodological and ideological view is voiced by the younger scholar Dr Miller, who represents the new breed of Orientalist: the 'post modernist', or 'new historian', and the post colonial. Dr Miller sees the root of the present situation in the struggle of the Palestinians who are rising against colonial rule after 100 years. National identity is seen as being an outdated, fictitious, imagined concept.[37] His ideas read like a lecture, artificially woven into the text:

> National identity was not a natural or empirical given, there being no such thing. It was a fictive construct used by the power structure to enslave the population it purportedly described ... National identity was an illegitimate concept even in a country like Israel that still pretended, albeit with increasing difficulty, to be democratic. Rather than let people decide for themselves who they were and how they wished to be defined, it trapped them in a rigid category that had no room for change, development, personal experience, or multiple identities. (pp.412–13)

On the surface these are seemingly radical ideas, yet at the same time Dr Miller is voicing the ancient and conventional view that regards the Arabs in ethnic and tribal terms: 'Surely Professor Rivlin was aware that beneath the tinsel of national identity ... there was something more genuine and primitive. The Arabs were too fluid and unbounded to be subsumed under a single national grid' (p.414).

The novel ends with Rivlin coming to terms with some of his private ghosts. He gives up his obsession concerning his son's divorce, and unlike the readers perhaps, he accepts the fact that he will never get to know the full story. Subsequently he 'meets' the reincarnation of his mother, whom he finds in the image of an elderly neighbour and to whom he refers as a 'ghost'. Significantly, the closing words of the novel are addressed to this 'ghost': 'You don't know me from anywhere. But now, ma'am, if you don't mind my saying so, you do know me a little bit' (p.568). It seems that Yehoshua is suggesting that in order to be able to understand the culture of the 'other' there is a need first of all to have a real confrontation with the ghosts of one's own culture, in this case with the dead parents of the previous generation. This may be the Dybbuk that is chasing the Israelis and which makes it impossible for them to see clearly not only the self, but also the other.

Understanding the self is the first step towards understanding the other. As far as the Israelis are concerned, Yehoshua seems to find an insight in Agnon's writings. In an interview with Yotam Reuveni, Yehoshua suggests that the Jewish roots in Agnon's writings threaten Zionist culture:

because of the fact that his protagonists struggled to keep their identity and their morality within a very clear religious system ... After the Zionist and socialist ideologies were shaken, it was important for us to see how such struggles are taking place within complete ancient Jewish systems ... because they pointed, for better and for worse, to wider and deeper roots of our identity, dangerous roots at times, that we had to know so that we could navigate our national independence, which is so new and revolutionary in Jewish history, and which produced new problems of identity which we did not know about beforehand.[38]

Agnon's texts represent cultural taboos as well as the possibility of liberation from provincial ties.[39] Similarly, Yehoshua's novel reflects the Dybbuk and other 'ghosts' from Jewish civilization on the one hand and the attempt to be liberated from them on the other. It also bravely attempts to cross the borders of one culture to the threshold of the civilization of the other and thereby avoid the clash of civilizations.

NOTES

1. A.B. Yehoshua, *Hakalah Ha-meshachreret* (Tel Aviv: Hakibbutz Hameuchad, 2001). Quotations are from the English translation (by Hillel Halkin), *The Liberated Bride* (London: Peter Halban, 2003).
2. Samuel P. Huntington, *The Clash of Civilizations and the Remaking of World Order* (London and New York: Touchstone Books, 1998), p.128.
3. Samuel Huntington, 'The Clash of Civilizations? The Debate', *Foreign Affairs* (1996), p.1. This article precedes the extended argument in Huntington, *The Clash of Civilizations and the Remaking of World Order*.
4. Huntington, 'The Clash of Civilizations?', p.4.
5. *The Jerusalem Report*, 12 July 2004, p.13.
6. Risa Domb, *The Arab in Hebrew Prose* (London and Portland, OR: Vallentine Mitchell, 1982).
7. Huntington, 'The Clash of Civilizations?', p.66.
8. This was explained by A.B. Yehoshua in his paper delivered at a conference held in Venice in his honour 18–21 April, 2005.
9. Yotam Reuveni, *Abraham B. Yehoshua, Two Interviews and Notes by Yotam Reuveni* (Rishon Letsion: Nimrod, 2003), p.82.
10. Very often the characters are not referred to by their names, but rather by their professions: the orientalist, the scholar, the son, and so on. This distances them from the narrator.
11. It seems interesting to note that Shlomo Zand observed that between 2001 and 2002 there appeared three Israeli novels in which the protagonists are historians: A.B. Yehoshua *The Liberated Bride*, Eyal Megged *The Dark Light*, and Avner Dankner *The Man with No Bones*. He suggests that their portrayal attempts to stabilize the collective memory which was shaped by these historians. See 'The Historian, Time and Imagination – the Portrayal of the Historian as a Literary Hero', *Maariv*, 28 Dec. 2004.
12. Samaher means 'spear, javelin, bayonet' according to Professor Rivlin and 'lance, spear' according to Rashid.
13. Lillian Dabby-Joury, 'Original and Translation: A Study of the Novel *The Liberating Bride*', *Alei Siach* 47 (Summer 2002), pp.55–67.
14. Reuveni, *Abraham B. Yehoshua, Two Interviews and Notes by Yotam Reuveni*, p.51.
15. A.B. Yehoshua, *A Journey To the End of the Millennium* (Tel Aviv: Hakibbutz Hameuchad, 1997).
16. For a wider discussion on this see Roland Barthes, 'The Discourse of History', in Michael Lane (ed.), *Structuralism: A Reader* (London: Cape, 1970), pp.145–55.

17. Bialik translated the play into Hebrew in *Ha-tekufah*, vol.1, (1918). For more on this see Nahma Sandrow, *Vagabond Stars: The World History of Yiddish Theatre* (New York: Harper & Row, 1977), p.217.
18. Hannah Tedeschi is another 'bride' who is 'liberated' from her husband and teacher when he dies.
19. Reuveni, *Abraham B. Yehoshua, Two Interviews and Notes by Yotam Reuveni*, p.78.
20. Rachel Albeck-Gidron, 'Totem and Blindness in Israel of 2001' (Unpublished paper), p.14.
21. Gil Eyal, *Avraham B. Yehoshua:* The Liberating Bride (Tel Aviv: Hakibbutz Hameuchad, 2001), pp.5–184.
22. Genesis 12.1.
23. See p.421 of the Hebrew edition. Interestingly, this is missing in the English translation.
24. Vikram Seth, *A Suitable Boy* (London: Phoenix, 1994).
25. Reuveni, *Abraham B. Yehoshua, Two Interviews and Notes by Yotam Reuveni*, p.69.
26. It appears overtly here, too: Rivlin finally writes something about Algeria when his spectacles are broken, but his vision remains blurred when it comes to his son's affair.
27. In this respect I disagree with Oren's insistence that any crossing of borders is dangerous, including the enforced crossing of cultural boundaries between the Israelis and Palestinians, which seems to lead both peoples to madness. Yosef Oren, *Hakol ha-gavri basipporet ha-Israelit* [The Male Voice in Israeli Prose] (Rishon Letsion: Yahad, 2002), pp.113–14.
28. Reuveni, *Abraham B. Yehoshua, Two Interviews and Notes by Yotam Reuveni*, p.44.
29. Ibid., p.45.
30. Ibid., p.46.
31. For more on the language of Islam see Navid Kermani, 'Silent Sirens', *TLS* (1 October 2004), pp.12–15.
32. The Israeli Arab, Naim Araidy, suggested that Yehoshua's appreciation of Arabic language and culture marks a higher level of Israeli culture. See his article 'The Liberating Language – A Study of the Novel *The Liberating Bride* by A.B. Yehoshua', *Dimooy*, 23 (2004), p.41.
33. It has been suggested by Yaakov Bar Siman-Tov that of the five Orientalists who appear in the novel, four are prejudiced against the Arabs in their research and Rivlin is the most authentic one. See the proceedings of the conference held in January 2002 at the Middle East Department at the Hebrew University entitled:' Orientalism and Academia: Chained or Liberated?', p.5. On that occasion Aharon Layish pointed to an autobiographical aspect of the choice of an Orientalist by Yehoshua: his father failed to get the support of Professor Bennet to write a PhD (p.3).
34. The other brides are Galya who possibly liberated, or was liberated by, Ofer, but maybe more so by her father's death. Samaher attempted to liberate herself from her marriage and escape into her mental condition.
35. See Oren, op.cit. p.111.
36. For an extensive study on this idea see Martin S. Alexander, Martin Evans and John F.V. Keiger, *The Algerian War and the French Army, 1954–1962: Experiences, Images, Testimonies* (Basingstoke: Palgrave Macmillan, 2002).
37. Echoing the idea of Benedict Anderson in his book *Imagined Communities* (London: Verso, 1991).
38. Reuveni, *Abraham B. Yehoshua, Two Interviews and Notes by Yotam Reuveni*, p.30.
39. See the conversation between Yoel and Rivlin (pp.468–9) with reference to Agnon's *The Bridal Canopy.*

8

Nothing Is As It Was: Time and Change in *Heatwave and Crazy Birds* by Gabriela Avigur-Rotem[1]

'Every few years a book appears which makes one feel that something extraordinary or even unique has happened. It struck me, as I completed Gabriela Avigur-Rotem's novel, that this is one of the ten texts written in Hebrew over the past decade which I would choose to take to a desert island.'[2] Professor Gershon Shaked's response was echoed by many critics[3] and readers. Not surprisingly, sales soared soon after the book's publication, even though it pre-dated the days of extravagant media campaigns, remaining high on the bestseller list for several months. The book is striking both in its form and content, its power coming from its simplicity and the beauty of the writing. The title's heatwaves and 'crazy birds' – a Yiddishism for 'madmen' – stand as metaphors for the essence of Israel as perceived by Avigur-Rotem. The proposition is focused and straightforward: the main protagonist, Loya, aged 48 and unmarried, returns to her childhood home after over twenty-five years abroad, providing the author with a vantage point from which to criticize changes within society. In this way she charts the shaping of Israeli identity over the course of time.

This temporal device parallels the spatial one used by writers of the 1980s, in which a physical journey often serves as a metaphor for a psychic flight and a search for self-identity, a phenomenon noted in *Home Thoughts from Abroad* (see also pp.4 and 32).[4] A.B. Yehoshua, for example, describes how the distance he set between himself and Israel during his stay in Paris in 1963–67 'seemed to help me accept Israeli reality',[5] revealing less of the 'other' in this case than of the self.

Amnon Rubinstein describes foreign travel as a device for putting Sabra culture under scrutiny, since it is easier to 'rediscover the lost conceptual paradise of Tel Aviv' from an external vantage point[6] which highlights the differences between 'inside' and 'outside'.[7]

By adding the temporal dimension, Avigur-Rotem provides us with another vantage point from which to view the development of Israeli identity. It has been pointed out that she 'has closely examined the overall condition of Israeli identity, producing a literary work at once internal and external, emphatic and critical, rich and severe, sharp and enjoyable ... This is not an "autopsy", but, ultimately, a ... courageous literary confrontation with ourselves.'[8] In order to do this, she explained, she:

> wanted the protagonist to be a woman who comes back after many years, so that everything that went wrong here would be totally obvious to her ... The Zionist base we tried to build is riddled with cracks and is doomed to destruction. The materials beneath the roots of the tree, [the parts] below the house, will destroy it. In the fifty-four years of Israel's existence more Jews have been killed here than anywhere else in the world. So what did we accomplish? Did we discover a wise solution? In this book I scrutinize that question.[9]

Avigur-Rotem suggests elsewhere in the same lecture, in discussing this book, that the journey to Loya Kaplan's past – to her particular type of psychology, to the one searing failure in her love-life (the impossibility of a relationship with her half-brother), which determines the fate of all subsequent relationships and brings about her emotional aridness – is also a journey into Israel as it once was. It is an odyssey into the settlement movement of the 1950s and 1960s and the story of her generation, born in the mid-1940s.[10]

In her first novel, *Mozart Was Not a Jew*,[11] she depicted the alienation of East European Jews in South America and their connection to the emerging national centre in Israel as one resolution for Jews in the twentieth century. Here, she examines the immigrant society that developed in Israel. 'Here in the harsh blue light – as the writer Amos Oz calls the Israeli experience – here everything was supposed to happen patriotically, economically, sanely, with purpose.'[12] Avigur-Rotem compares Israel soon after its establishment with the country some fifty years on, using the past to reveal the present. Memory is therefore the pivot around which the novel revolves, as she describes a generation that appears to have created its own culture and social behaviour. Although all generations do this to an extent, in this particular case there was a more deliberate and dramatic sloughing off of the past and a plucking of a new identity as if from the air. This is reinforced by the book's epigraph from a poem by Yehuda Amichai,[13] which claims that the winners in life, if there are any, are those who remember their childhood. But she shows also how this new society failed to internalize the Zionist ideals on which it was established, or the memories of the Holocaust which preceded its founding. Israelis in the 1950s constructed their sense of 'self' from the 'here-and-now', preferring to draw on the Bible for its memories rather than on the recent past. Avigur-Rotem suggests that this denial of memory undermined the foundations on which the State of Israel was created, leaving a soulless core.

The temporal dimension operates from the opening pages, establishing a style in which several time-scales run in parallel. The protagonist reconstructs in her mind dialogues remembered from childhood, using children's vernacular of the 1940s or 1950s,[14] interspersed with remarks made by a lawyer in 1994, the time of narration, while her thoughts drift to still other periods. She recalls her relationship in Paris with a frightened Jean-Jacques, whom she meets while working as an air-hostess, an episode which unfolds as her memory shifts back and forth throughout the novel, some time-shifts being so slight that the reader is unsure which period is being referred to, mirroring in effect what is happening to its protagonist. The emotional baggage Loya brings with her is continually colliding with the reality of the present, and the more she encounters the present, the greater her nostalgia for the past. But to some extent, it is a past that never entirely existed.

Nostalgia plays an important role in the novel and indeed, much has been said of the link between the notion of nostalgia and one's homeland. According to Linda Hutcheon:

> Simultaneously distancing and proximating, nostalgia exiles us from the present as it brings the imagined past near. The simple, pure, ordered, easy, beautiful, or harmonious past is constructed (and then experienced emotionally) in conjunction with the present – which, in turn, is constructed as complicated, contaminated, anarchic, difficult, ugly, and confrontational ... The aesthetics of nostalgia might, therefore, be less a matter of simple memory than of complex projection; the invocation of a partial, idealized history merges with a dissatisfaction with the present. And it can do so with great force.[15]

Loya's nostalgia, like that of Avigur-Rotem's herself, is clearly made all the more poignant by the particular time it recalls, when Israel was new and the Zionist dream was on the point of being realized, before harsh reality and disillusion set in.

As well as re-discovering her country, Loya also learns important information about her past, which is only divulged to the reader at the same time. For example, we are told quite late on in the novel that Loya (whose unusual name is a biblical Hebrew term for a building component drawn from *I Kings* 7:29–30) had been called Leah on her birth in Venice in 1946 on the way to Israel, the year Avigur-Rotem was also born.[16] She also arrives in Israel at the same time as had Avigur-Rotem, in January 1950.[17] Loya assumes that her mother, Milena, whom she has not seen for many years, is dead, but she now discovers that Milena had returned to Czechoslovakia after only a year in Israel, lured by the attractions of Communism, and that she had been arrested there on suspicion of espionage and imprisoned for fifteen years, unable to contact her family in Israel. Ironically, she had been a Communist activist and had left Israel for ideological reasons.

Loya has been raised by her father, a professor of archaeology at the Hebrew University of Jerusalem, and his friend Davidi, also an archaeologist, who has a son, Nahum. At first neither Nahum nor Loya know that they are half-brother and sister, both the children of Milena, and in fact, after Loya's father dies when she is 20, she and Nahum fly to Eilat and unexpectedly and – as it turns out – shockingly – make love, telling no one about it.

Loya has an unusual upbringing. She is familiar not only with the Bible, but with Greek mythology, Roman history, Phoenician legends and the discoveries at Qumran and Ugarit,[18] and lives in a house whose walls are covered with books. Her father is proud that at 6 she can write in ancient Hebrew script and that at 10 she can copy Y.L. Peretz's story 'Three Gifts' into hieroglyphs. Nearly every Saturday the four of them look for archaeological sites, searching for traces of life beneath the earth in the heat of the *hamsin*. Her father (Professor Otta Kaplan, though he is known throughout here almost entirely through his function as father to Loya) and Davidi find Roman coins, some of them later worth a fortune, as well as pottery and other objects. Otta insists she wear heavy hiking boots because of her flat feet, even though she wants delicate shoes like those of her friend Adriana. He wants her to remain with her feet firmly on the ground, both literally and metaphorically, rooted and connected to the soil in the pioneering manner of the early settlers. No one expects her to become only an air-hostess, but this enables both her literal and metaphorical flight from her past and her home country. Her return at the age of 48 is prompted by Davidi's death. She has been left to sell the house and to dispose of the phoenix-shaped urn containing his ashes,[19] since Nahum had died in a flying accident while serving in the army.

Loya expects her visit to be a short one, but she cannot tear herself away from fragments of her past. She reads letters and a diary kept by her father and discovers that her parents had been imprisoned in Terezin. She also discovers that Milena had become pregnant by Davidi while there, but that when he was about to be transferred to an extermination camp, Loya's father had agreed to marry Milena in order to save her and the unborn baby from being sent with Davidi. Nahum was therefore Loya's half-brother. Loya also learns that her mother might still be alive, and so travels to Terezin, only to find a 75-year-old Milena with whom she cannot establish any emotional contact. They do not kiss and 'have no common language' (p.367). Loya returns to Israel to find that the municipality has declared the foundations of Davidi's house unsafe and have begun demolishing it, much as Loya's foundations have crumbled in the wake of recent discoveries.

Alongside the impact of time, distance and memory on identity, language is no less important a factor for Avigur-Rotem. 'Writing is a way of paying homage to the instrument I play on: the Hebrew language',[20] she proclaimed after the publication of her first novel. Here also we are aware of her use of a rich, metaphoric, high-register Hebrew in which words assume extra weight and their sound underlines their meaning. An obvious example is that the title of the book, as well as each of the titles of the other ten chapters, gives prominence to the Hebrew letter *chet*, the first, for instance, being *Hamsin, Hasidot* ('Heatwave, Storks').[21] In fact, the triad of *Hevreh (*Friends), *Humus* and *Hamsin*, with the recurring letter *chet*, defines the essence of Israel, both in its throaty, emphatic and uncompromising sound, a sound that distinguishes the Hebrew language, and in representing three such significant elements of Israeli life.[22] 'Mr Humus, Israeli to the marrow, coarse, rough, full of good intentions, who knows everything better' (p.138). 'Hamsin, humus, hevreh, this is the story on one foot' (p.243). Another obvious way in which words and images assume extra function is in the frequent reference to birds.[23] Avigur-Rotem explains that 'the initial idea was to make the protagonist a photographer of birds ... Later her profession changed because I wanted her to come back to Israel after many years abroad. But the birds stayed.'[24] Gershon Shaked argues that the birds represent the precariousness of the heroine's existence, in which 'flight between heaven and earth resembles her migration, loving the crazy birds of her homeland but realizing that her nest might be an illusion'.[25] 'Whoever has wings – there are always possibilities' (p.17). At the same time, the birds, which have become wild, also represent nearly everyone who has become crazy in the neighbourhood of the protagonist's home.[26] Avigur-Rotem ironically suggests that 'you don't have to stretch wings to move from one place to another' (p.133).

The virtuoso-poetic style of the novel is integral to an imaginative world in which 'everything awakens to life, returns from words to sight' (p.133), to the extent that poetic syntax, rhythmic patterns and diction are essential to how the novel 'works'.[27] Some images, such as the seasonal changes that transform trees into a thicket (*sevach*) are suggestive, in this particular case of the binding of Isaac, while others are symbolic or metaphorical. A fig-tree which resembles a roaring lion with developed muscles and a huge dark top is cruelly cut down by a developer because its roots are undermining the house. This probably represents the State of Israel, apparently robust but with weak foundations. Another such tree buries the grocery shop owned by an elderly Holocaust survivor, probably hinting at the way the State has submerged the memory of the Holocaust in its foundations. Palm trees seem to threaten, with their thin trunks and blade-like leaves, while a citrus grove, so significant of early Statehood, is dried up, only one of a pair of Cyprus trees survives,[28] and even 'the Hibiscus looks at me with red eyes' (p.36). The author uses sensuous personifications: 'darkness is rustling, breathing heavily, scratching to get out' (p.11), 'darkness looks at us with scores of eyes' (p.16), 'a hiccup of water from the neck of the tap' (p.17), 'the whisper of the trolleys' (p.20), or 'I manage to release from the tap a cough, a sneeze and another cough' (p.21). She also uses synaesthesia, such as in speaking of 'a crimson chirp' (p.12), coffee with a 'mature, brown-purple smell' (p.21), 'the topographic rhythms of the earth' (p.151), 'unripe, stuttering Hamsin' (p.243); and has an affection for imaginative similes: 'every keyhole resembles a girl cut out of darkness; a huge head connected without a neck to a widening dress without hands, without feet' (p.12), or 'I was crawling on my belly, the stone is smooth, cool, closing on me like two slices of cheese' (p.16).

The author occasionally subverts meaning to draw attention to language, such as when she uses phrases lifted verbatim from children's games (for example, 'the vessels are broken and there is no play', p.112). She also occasionally lowers the register[29] or divides words incorrectly to reflect how they are spoken or sung.[30] Her adjectival phrases recall S. Yizhar,[31] drawing attention to the sound of words[32] and echoing the emphasis on foreign languages. Loya speaks many languages,[33] but realizes she knows Czech only after her arrival in Czechoslovakia, discovering that 'the forgotten language was revealed to her in small clumps' (p.356). Elsewhere she slips into air-hostess terminology – 'You may unfasten your safety belts. Smoking is permitted' (p.12) – or, after criticizing the way teachers no longer correct spelling mistakes,[34] continues to refer to her friend's mother childishly as *imashelora*, 'the mother of Ora' rather than 'Ora's mother'.

Avigur-Rotem also reproduces authentically different layers and styles of spoken Hebrew to underline the diverse origins of the people who made up Israeli society at the time. Her friend Shlomi's mother speaks the broken Hebrew of European immigrants, while Shlomi himself addresses his father 'in fluent Yiddish, like an old man from the Diaspora' (pp.19, 25), reflecting his dual association with the new world of Israel and with the old one despised by early Zionist society. Loya's father's letters from Terezin in 1939 are written in the Hebrew of someone for whom it is not a spoken language, and the elderly owner of the grocery shop makes grammatical errors, as do others.[35] Other period-specific elements are the snatches of popular songs of the time,[36] and the conversational style of old friends[37] or of the Yemenite taxi driver.[38] Davidi, Loya notes, is interested in the origins of words, making this aspect of the novel a homage to him. Awareness of language is occasionally deployed to humorous effect, such as in the comically exaggerated description of Jean-Jacques's fear of flying or the account of how the 'centre' of town has moved. In one portrait of hypocrisy one hears how 'the whole year he steals sharpeners and erasers from satchels, copies during exams, but on Yom Kippur, like a righteous man, goes to synagogue' (p.40).[39]

Avigur-Rotems's examination of the linguistic changes that took place during the first fifty-four years of Israel's existence provides the framework for a much wider evaluation of self and identity. Loya finds that 'nothing is as it was' (p.84). The neighbourhood now has a shopping centre, many houses have acquired extensions, their well-tended front gardens home to Persians cats and barking dogs. Of the changes to her own house she says, 'even the garden is different; of the large garden which was an orchard full of blossom and smells and fruit and shadows, a handkerchief-size lawn is left and a row of stiff flowers, devoid of joy' (p.102). Nostalgically, when she buys flowers she chooses species she remembers from her childhood rather than the now popular exotic plants.

Another disappointing change has occurred in kibbutz life. Loya is shocked when she visits her first boyfriend's kibbutz for the first time in thirty years, to find that this stronghold of socialist idealism is now far larger than it was and that no one has heard of him. A member comments: 'Once everyone used to know everyone – and now ... now no one sees further than his own belly button' (p.93). Manners have also changed. When she holds out her hand to Bilu, her old school friend, he does not shake it as he used to do, but in a more sophisticated and less meaningful manner he 'bends down and gives me a wet kiss on my cheek. A new custom has come to the country; and now the second cheek' (p.26). When she asks in a shop for the sandals that were popular in her childhood the shopkeeper asks acidly 'Where have you been living?' (p.13). She also notes the common use of the Hamsa (five-fingered sign) against the evil eye, as though 'everyone's a complete pagan' (p.136). The names of streets and even of neighbourhoods have changed, replacing historical associations with the names of flowers[40] in an overt and conscious effort to reject and overthrow the past, even to cover it up and erase it. Names altogether played a major role in the Israeli reconstruction of self, as Loya notes: 'We made such a thing of names – no one was satisfied – everyone was jealous of the name given to someone else' (p.28). Loya's childhood friends, many of them named for deceased relatives, dream of changing their own: 'Marganit was named after Marina and Nita; Tsafrira after Tsipora and Mira; Reudor after Reuven and Theodor; but best of all was Minaleh – Mina for Miriam, and then Yentel, Niuta, Hinde' (p.29). She is surprised to find that she had been born Leah. Ora's mother was named Mechora after the last word of the chorus of a popular Zionist song: '*Ma od tevakshi me-itanoo mechora*' (What else will you ask of us oh Homeland) (p.35). Some names were once associated with sites of heroism – Yodefet, Metsada, Ghil'ad or Efrat – while others, such as Shmuel, Rahamim and Moshe, were given to children of Oriental origin. But now the children have non-exilic biblical names not used by the shtetl Jews, such as Datan, Omri or Ahaz, while Loya's childhood friend Shlomi, a professor of Yiddish in New Jersey, has become Shlom-'ami. There is also a trend for naming children after characters of whom the biblical prophets did not approve. Davidi's first name is Barak, after an Israelite hero, and his nickname for Loya is Anat, after the pagan goddess. This reflects a shift in attitudes towards an antiexilic existence, a notion reinforced by Davidi's belief that 'We are all Canaanites. Our prophets wanted us to be the chosen people, but we should have integrated into the Semitic surroundings' (p.59). He is not in favour of negating Jewish specificity – 'Hebrew is the sky above us – Hebrew is the air – Hebrew is also the wind' (p.129) – but he leaves directions for a non-religious funeral in which no one will mumble thanks to God. Loya's friend Adriana reports that Davidi has left her the house to lure her back, but by dispersing his ashes over the ruins of the city of Beitar Loya dissolves the Canaanite option. However, she stays nonetheless (see also pp.18–19).

Central to the novel are the changes undergone by Loya's contemporaries, a cross-section of Israeli society of the 1950s. Tikva, the only Oriental Jew in the circle (and the only Oriental character in the novel, other than a marginal character who is a Yemenite taxi driver), is elegant, married and a deputy manager in a local bank. Yosefa has become a lawyer, drives a BMW and believes that she and her friends are representative of typical Israeli society. She claims to be 'up to date on who is a grandmother, whose son got killed in Lebanon or was severely wounded during the *intifada,* how many got divorced and how many got married-divorced-remarried and so on, and who is rich or famous' (p.65). In this society, the death of young soldiers has become a 'normal' fact of life. Shockingly, parents still take it for granted that they must sacrifice their children to the State. Yosefa irritates Loya, who notes that whereas they used to discuss happiness, now their conversations are about 'children? Health? Have you finished renovating? How was it abroad?' (pp.166–7). No one has turned out as they thought they would, and all have become older, domesticated and more materialistic. Many Israelis travel and children study computing at school rather than the work of the classical poet Tchernikhovsky. As children Loya and her friends knew his work by heart and used to admire him, but he has been forgotten. Another regrettable change is that only elementary-school teachers and the Orthodox mention the Hebrew months. But the changes that have taken place in Ora – beautiful, tall and Loya's best friend – are the most painful. She had been a model child, the best pupil in class, helpful to friends and a volunteer in border kibbutzim. She even went to synagogue on festivals, although she belonged to the extreme-left-wing (and by implication, secular) Hashomer Hatsa'ir youth movement. Loya very much wishes to seek her out, thinking that time cannot separate them, but is too nervous to do so at first and instead addresses her in a stream-of-consciousness recollection of closeness.[41] Yet when she eventually meets Ora after thirty-three years she is shocked and disappointed to find her unattractive, worn out, 'heavy, but dressed loosely to hide how much so, her hair short, thin, dyed aubergine-black, her face sweating, her eyes – a half risen sun surrounded by grey halo – Ora!? It is not possible, not like that' (p.71). Loya tries not to cry. Apparently Ora is a teacher, and Loya wonders what she sees in her undistinguished husband. But she is a busy mother of four children and looks after her aging parents. To Loya, she is simply jaded, like the country.

Avigur-Rotem recalls the cultural components that contributed to the shaping of Israeli identity, such as cinema, books, language and festivals. Cinema used to be the only entertainment for children in the

1950s and served as a window on the outside world. Accordingly, Loya's memories of childhood include many references to cinema,[42] from films popular at the time, such as *Ivanhoe*, *The Bicycle Thieves* and *La Dolce Vita*, as well as to the much admired actress Sophia Loren. Indeed, she used to operate the Hebrew subtitles shown with films in the local community centre. There are also references to popular books such as Thor Heyerdahl's *The Kon Tiki Expedition*, Y. Mossenshon's *Hasamba*, Victor Hugo's *Les Miserables*, Romain Rolland's *Jean-Christophe* and Nikos Kazantzakis's *Zorba the Greek*. Loya's Hebrew is fossilized and she uses dated expressions such as *tsarchaniya* for a grocery shop, while Mina's mother uses the term 'rice' stitch for her knitting. The knickerbockers worn by Loya's father and Davidi are 'Zalman trousers' (p.36), and there are references to Biedermeier furniture brought from Europe, popular games,[43] school nurses examining girls' hair for nits and the voice of the popular radio announcer Re'umah Eldar. One hears of fashion-conscious boys parading in front of the cinema 'with falling quiff, loosened sandals, shorts tucked up to show the pockets ... and girls with wide elasticated belts over wide, blown-up skirts' (p.94), emphasizing a world that is utterly past and inaccessible, one whose traces can barely even be seen in the present.

Central to Loya's experience of childhood had been the Jewish festivals. She contrasts the present bustling atmosphere on the eve of the Jewish New Year with the intimacy of the past: 'The new centre is full of people – where were they a week ago? – laden trolleys, queues, saleswomen offering wine to taste, soup, apple-flavoured honey. But I hug with both hands the fan I have just bought and look at the queue to the left: strangers, strangers, strangers looking through me, not one familiar face, not even one who coughs or clears a throat to attract my attention and ask for water, coffee, a newspaper, earphones. I am not needed by anybody. Wonderful. Terrible. I can do whatever I want. Wonderful. What do I want' (pp.17–18). The simple celebration of *Sukkot* (the Feast of Tabernacles) has lost its significance and became just like any other typical Israeli party: 'It is hot, very hot, scorching, boiling – thirty, no, forty people sitting closely around tables laden with humus, pita bread, pickles, falafel balls, thinly sliced salad, mounds of pickled cabbage and hills of olives and, every few meters, the drinks: Coke, Diet Coke, Kinley, Sprite, orange drink – and arms stretched to reach, crossing, pinching half a pita bread' (p.70). On Independence Day there had once been crowds in the streets, folk-dancing, fireworks and a military parade. Nowadays, although singing is still practiced, it is celebrated in private with barbeques, and the usual humus and pita.

Another unwelcome change is that even this attenuated celebration is compromised by a recent terrorist attack in which people are killed. The fear is that the next 'might be in Jerusalem ... or Tel Aviv, in a central place – at the Cultural Hall, Dizengoff Centre. Why not in Givata'im or Holon?' (p.331). Israelis have good reason to talk politics and express concerns for their security. 'This is a land which eats up its inhabitants' (p.246, citing *Numbers* 13:32), which may be one of the reasons why many now go abroad with their families for the festivals, like migrating birds. Not only to escape the cooking and chaos, but because people are tired and 'run away to rest a little' (p.84). The younger generation has no patience even for the Passover *Haggadah* (the tale of the Exodus read on Passover night), and *Purim* (the Festival of Lots) has changed beyond recognition. It seems that the only festival to have survived without changes is the Day of Atonement, *Yom Kippur*, which, because it was the most solemn day in the calendar for adults, who spent the time in prayer, usually meant a day of freedom for children, without adults, meals, cars or danger.

The Holocaust is a constant presence in Loya's childhood, represented most obviously by the elderly shopkeeper with the tattooed arm who speaks Hebrew laced with Yiddishisms. The children, haunted by the secrets kept from them about the Holocaust feel that they have to prepare themselves for the worst. They build for themselves a secret bunker in the outskirts of the settlement where they store 'candles, nails, rags, empty bottles, matches, in case the Nazis come, in case the Arabs come to throw women and infants into the sea, we were prepared' (p.18). They are bent on 'preparing against the Arabs so that the Nazis would not make soap out of them' (p.37). The threat from Nazis and Arabs become intertwined in their imagination as one and the same. Although their parents do not mention the Holocaust to the children, its memory is manifested in unexpected ways. Loya's father exclaims: 'We don't light memorial candles, we don't pray and we don't hold any pagan ritual. We are modern people' (p.58). Despite his efforts to forget, simply building a bonfire on the shores of Lake Kinneret reminds him of the horrors of the gas chambers: 'flesh burns, fat – fat burns very well' (p.21). Shlomi's mother, a survivor, hoards in her wardrobe 'five or six drawers containing loaves of bread one on top of the other, just like the grocery shop, this is the cemetery of the bread' (p.26). She cannot recover from the trauma of the Holocaust. But the past is kept well submerged. When Ora's mother asks if they had been taught about the Holocaust at school, Loya says they had not, but that the children had heard stories from survivors and that more came out during the Eichmann trial. The children learn much about the Holocaust and its repercussions from their immediate families, friends and neighbours. No family had been left untouched: Ora is shocked to discover by chance from old photographs that her father, who used to light thirty-six memorial candles at home for his entire family, had been married before, and Loya identifies a visitor from America as Ora's half-brother by a German mother. Loya observes that none of her generation has a living grandmother. Only the Oriental Tikva has a huge family, the Sephardim (or Orientals) having suffered far fewer casualties than the Ashkenazi Jews. Tikva has 'strange' customs that are despised by Ora's mother who voices the view of the Ashkenazi immigrants: 'No wonder they breed criminals' (p.29). Tikva's mother looks different, and they have 'different food, overwhelming, even the rice, even the meat cutlets, even the tea – very sweet, very dark, with its floating mint-leaf boats' (p.69). Only when they grow up do they begin to be interested in the Holocaust and as an adult Loya learns much from viewing Claude Landsmann's film *Shoah*, nine hours of testimony from witnesses, victims and participants of the Holocaust.[44] Ora's brother-in-law Avi, a historian of the Holocaust period who interviews survivors in Loya's neighbourhood for their testimonies, including Davidi before his death, informs her that her father had been in Terezin and that Davidi had been sent in 1942 to Treblinka, from where few returned. Her father had told her little, not even that Davidi had been his student in Prague. It is these revelations – and the sense that there is much more to find out – that prompt her to ask Avi to find out more about her mother. Ultimately, Loya decides to stay, her suitcase physically lighter once she has scattered Davidi's ashes, but she has also shed much personal baggage, and to some extent, come to terms with her past, perhaps accepting the inevitable impact time has on memory.

In conclusion, Avigur-Rotem compares the Israeli identity inspired by Zionist ideology in the early stage of Statehood with the reality that emerged over time. Her nostalgia for childhood is tinged with criticism, especially for the way the Holocaust had been a taboo subject, distorting children's view of Jewish history. Ashkenazi dominance is also evident from the fact that there is only one Oriental character, Tikva, and that her family is mistrusted. The central protagonist, Loya, appears disappointed by her contemporaries' mediocre achievements and preoccupation with material things, domesticity and physical aging. Little seems to have changed in the relations between the childhood friends, and there is a sense of stagnation. Loya is particularly struck by the way Israeli identity has shed distinctive Jewish features in adopting Western behaviour and values.

The realities of the present appear in a particularly harsh light when set against the nostalgic, rosy glow of the past, but nevertheless, the fact remains that something has been lost since the heady days of the Establishment of the State of Israel, which was founded on Zionist ideology and which united disparate people in a common cause. Ironically, as the State became established and the immediate threats to security and basic livelihood receded, smaller divisions and squabbles set in, which deepened with the next generation, who were also intent on shedding the baggage of the past which weighed so heavily around their necks. But in doing so, perhaps they also lost something vital, to their souls and to the country as a whole. Avigur-Rotem seems to be pleading for a healthy balance between acknowledging and incorporating the past in the present without being paralysed by it: It was said of the stars 'All that we see now is not what there is now, but that which has been – what we see now is history' (p.330). Perhaps this is true also of Israeli society. The evolution and shaping of Israeli identity is the result of the past and is determined by education, ideals and priorities. Perhaps it is not too late to find a positive way forward.

NOTES

1. Gabriela Avigur-Rotem, *Heatwave and Crazy Birds* (Tel Aviv: Keshet, 2001).
2. Gershon Shaked, 'In Praise of the Hamsin', *Yediot Aharonot*, 10 August 2001.
3. Critics such as Rochelle Furstenberg (in *Modern Hebrew Literature*), Yehudit Orian, Batya Gur and Avner Shatz (in *Ha'aretz*), Yael Paz-Melamed (in *Ma'ariv*), Jon Fedder in an interview, the book's editor Professor Yigal Schwartz (Keter Publishing House).
4. Risa Domb, *Home Thoughts from Abroad* (London and Portland, OR: Valentine Mitchell, 1995).
5. Cited by Joseph Cohen, *Voices of Israel* (New York: State University of New York Press, 1990), p.47.
6. Amnon Rubinstein, *Liheyot 'am hofshi* [To be a Free People] (Jerusalem and Tel Aviv: Schocken, 1977), p.112.
7. Using the terminology of Gaston Bachelard in *The Poetics of Space* (Boston: Beacon Press, 1969), pp.211–16.
8. See Yoram Melzer, *Ma'ariv*, 25 May 2001.
9. Avigur-Rotem, in a lecture delivered at Beit Ariela in Tel Aviv, Dec. 2001.
10. Avigur-Rotem, in a lecture delivered at Beit Ariela mentioned above.
11. Gabriela Avigur-Rotem, *Mozart Was Not a Jew* (Jerusalem: Keter, 1992).
12. From a lecture delivered at the 11th World Jewish Congress, Jerusalem, 24 June 1993.
13. ...When I think about humanity
    I think only of those born around the same time as me...
    You are all the brothers of my hopes
    And friends of my despair.
    He who remembers his childhood
    More than others is the winner
    If there are winners at all
    Taken from '1924' by Yehuda Amichai, in *She'at ha-hesed* (Tel Aviv: Schocken, 1982), pp.69–70, translated by Risa Domb.
14. See, for example, p.155.
15. Linda Hutcheon, *Irony, Nostalgia and the Postmodern* (1997), available at http://www.library.utoronto.ca/criticism/hutchiup.html.
16. Born in Buenos Aires, Argentina, Avigur-Rotem arrived in Israel in 1950. She received the

Peter Schwisert Prize for Young Writers and the Tel Aviv Rabinovich Prize for her poetry collection entitled *Walls and Emperors*. She was also awarded the 1992 Prime Minister Award for her novel *Mozart Was Not a Jew*.
17. See pp.144, 287.
18. For example, pp.19, 23, 31, 33, 43–4, 45, 77–8, 86, 105, 107, 113–14, 120, 162, 261.
19. See pp.37, 336.
20. From a lecture delivered at the World Jewish Congress, 24 June 1993.
21. *Hevreh, Humus, Heshvan ve-hatsavim* (p.53), *Harasim ve-Halomot* (p.96), *Hanukah* (p.125), *Halon ba-Horef* (p.153), *Hashrah* (p.187), *Ham, Ham Yoter, Ham Me'od* (p.213), *Harichah* (p.241), *Homa Adoomah* (p.259), *Hai* (p.309), *Hatimah* (p.347). See also pp.61–2, 243.
22. See pp.171, 243.
23. For example, pp.12, 28, 32, 38, 44, 49, 61, 76, 85, 94–5, 110, 115, 135, 226, 338.
24. Lecture delivered at Beit Ariela.
25. Shaked, 'In Praise of the Hamsin'.
26. See pp.23, 25, 37, 62.
27. See for example the fine descriptions of a flight on p.342, a desert landscape on p.345 and others on pp.61, 65 and 320. For more on the elements of poetic language see Winfred Nowottny, *The Language Poets Use* (London: Athlone Press, 1984), pp.1–25.
28. See pp.7, 8, 9.
29. For example, pp.141, 324.
30. For example, pp.134, 143, 206, 232.
31. For example, pp.129, 140, 147, 173.
32. For example, p.131.
33. For example, p.127.
34. See p.134.
35. For example, pp.19, 23 and 20, 22.
36. For example, pp.329, 335, 336, 346.
37. For example, pp.330–1, 336.
38. See p.369.
39. Other such comic interludes appear on pp.28, 134, 143, 194 and 206.
40. See pp.14, 27, 65, 79.
41. For example, pp.24, 36, 94, 217.
43. For example, pp.40, 87.
44. The importance and centrality of this documentary film in the novel is testified by the extensive description stretching over six whole pages (pp.247–52).

Index

A Dream Come True (E. Ben-Yehuda), 14
A Tale of Love and Darkness (A. Oz), 59
Adorno, Theodor, 22, 25, 61
Age of Revival (1880–1920), 12, 13, 15
Agnon, S.Y., 2, 17–19, 70, 87, 88
Akri, Efraim, 86
Al-Rashid Street, 68
Aleichem, Scholem, 75
Alexander III, 2
Algeria, War of Independence/Revolution, 80, 86
Alroi, Yosef, 37
Amichai, Yehuda, 14, 92
Amir, Eli, 69
'An Important Question' (E. Ben-Yehuda), 13–14
Anderson, Benedict, 2
Anski, S., 82
Appelfeld, Aharon, birth, 57; identity problems, 63–4; and language, 62–3, 74; life writing, 60; and Sami Michael, 70; Poetics of Silence, 61; *Story of a Life*, 3, 57–66; wartime experiences, 57, 60–1, 64
Arab in Hebrew Prose, 79
Arab–Israeli conflict, 47
Arabian Peninsula, 85–6
Around the Point (Y.H. Brenner), 14–15, 17
arts, comparison between, 27–8; and ideology, 29–31, 33; television productions as art form, 26–7
Ashkenazim, 3, 67; and Iraqi Jews, 71
Asides (S. Yizhar), 59
Aunt Shlomtsion the Queen (Y. Kaniuk), 39, 43, 44–5
Auschwitz, 61
autobiographies, 58, 59
Avigur-Rotem, Gabriela, 3, 4, 17, 90–103; on language, 95–6
Avishai, M., 37

Balas, Shimon, 69
Band, Arnold, 20
Barabash, B., 17
Barartsion, 46
Barthes, Roland, 26
Beckett, Samuel, 4
Be'er, Haim, 59
Begin, Menahem, 5
Be'mo Yadav (Pirkey Elik), 51
Ben-Yehuda, Eliezer, 13–14
Benjamin, Walter, 28–9
Berdichevsky, M.Y., 13, 15
Berg, Nancy, 68–9
Bergner, Yossel, 64
Bialik, H.M., 13, 21
bilingualism, 80
biographies, 58
Blatt, Avraham, 37
Borrowed Name (M. Megged), 59
Brenner, Joseph Hayyim, 2, 14–15, 17, 58, 69
Bronowski, Yoram, 20–1
Buber, Martin, 64
Bundestaag, visit by Weitzman (1996), 11
Burstein, Dror, 64
By the Sea (S. Yizhar), 59

camera obscura, 25
Camus, Albert, 4
Canaanite movement (1940s), 18–19
Castel-Bloom, O., 17
Celan, Paul, 61–2
Clash of Civilizations and the Remaking of World Order (S. Huntington), 78

da Vinci, Leonardo, 27
Dante, 44
Death of a Donkey (Y. Kaniuk), 39
Death of My Mother (N. Zach), 59
Deleuze, Gilles, 63
dialectical imagery, 25

Index

Divine Comedy (Dante), 44
Dolly City (O. Castel-Bloom), 17
Dryden, John, 27
Dybbuk (classical play), 80–1, 82, 83, 86, 88

Eagleton, Terry, 6, 22–3
Eldar, Re'umah, 99
Enlightenment, European, 14
Exile from Exile – Israeli Writers from Iraq (N. Berg), 68–9
Existentialism, 3–4

Fechter, Mordechai, 37
Feierberg, Mordecai Ze'ev, 14, 58, 69
Fertile Crescent, 18
First World War, and Jewish life, 59
'For Whom Do I Toil' (Y.L. Gordon), 12, 13
Frankfurt school, 22, 25
Fugitive Pieces (A. Michaels), 62

Games of Loneliness (N. Zarhi), 59
Gaza, 86
'Generation of the State' writers, 59
Ghosh, Abu, 85
Ginath (scholar), 18, 19
Gnessin, U.N., 13
Goertz, Nurit, 45
Goldvich, Michal, 60
Gordon, Y.L., 12, 13
Great Madness (A. Hameiri), 59
Guattari, Felix, 63

Ha-Am, Ahad, 13
Ha-Shahar, 12
Hagorni, Avraham, 37
Hagorni, Yosef, 37
Halachic Judaism, 19
Hall, Stuart, 5, 36
Hameiri, Avigdor, 59
Hasamba (Y. Mossenshon), 99
Hashomer Hatsa'ir youth movement, 98
Hasidism, 54
Haskalah (Jewish Enlightenment movement), 12, 13, 58
Hatikvah (national anthem), 51
Heatwave and Crazy Birds (G. Avigur-Rotem), 3, 4, 17, 90–103; characterization/plot, 91, 92–102; virtuoso-poetic style, 95, *see also* Avigur-Rotem, Gabriela
Hebrew language, 1, 3; Rabbinic Hebrew, as Aramaic syntax, 13; role in Jewish nationalism, 2; spoken, 16; written, 16
hegemony, religious, twentieth-century collapse, 58
Holocaust, Auschwitz, 61; as catalyst for change, 36; Celan's view of, 61–2; effects, 6, 64; and *Heatwave and Crazy Birds*, 100–1; Kaniuk on, 46, 47–9; and War of Independence (1948), 52; and Zionism, 71

Horace (commentator), 27
Howe, Irving, 26, 30, 33
Huntington, Samuel, 78, 79
Hutcheon, Linda, 92

iconoclasm, 25
identity, Appelfeld, problems of, 63–4; cultural, 22; Israeli/Jewish, 6, 22, 67–8, 73–4; Kaniuk on, 36; and language, 11–21
ideology/idealism, 3, 5, 11; and art, 29–31, 33; and novel, 30; as totalitarian system, 22; Zionist, 3, 5, 14, 16
Ido VeEnam (Ido and Enam) (S.Y. Agnon), 17–19
imagery, and words, 27, 28
In The Winter (J.H. Brenner), 58
intifada, 23, 79, 98
Ionesco, Eugene, 4
Israeli society, 25

Jean-Christophe (Romain Rolland), 99
Jewish time, Kaniuk on, 50
Journey to the End of the Millennium (A.B. Yehoshua), 5, 81

Kafka, Franz, 4, 63
Kaniuk, Yoram, 3; *Aunt Shlomtsion the Queen*, 39, 43, 44–5; *Death of a Donkey*, 39; on Holocaust, 46, 47–9; on identity, 35, 54; on Jewish time, 50; language, use of, 44; *Last Jew*, 36–56; *Post Mortem*, 43, 59; on Realism, 46; on War of Independence (1948), 38, 41–2, 45, 46, 47; writing style, 44
Kaplan, Otta, 93
Karpal, Dalya, 70, 73
kibbutz life, 96–7
Kinneret, Lake, 100
Kon Tiki Expedition (Thor Heyerdahl), 99
Kurtzweil, Baruch, 37

Landsmann, Claude, 101
language, Appelfeld's experiences, 62–3; Avigur-Rotem on, 95–6; and identity, 11–21, 31; and ideology, 11; Kaniuk's use of, 44; and nationalism, 31
Last Jew (Yoram Kaniuk), 3, 36–56; characterisation/plot, 37–45, 49–50, 51–3; Christianity in, 45; critical view of, 37, 45; influences on, 50; messianism in, 45; as stream of consciousness novel, 47; surreal nature of, 45, 46, *see also* Kaniuk, Yoram
Les Miserables (Victor Hugo), 99
le'umoot (nationalism), 14
Levi, Primo, 62
Liberating Bride (A. B. Yehoshua), 3, 78–89 characterization/plot, 79–84; *Dybbuk*, 80–1, 82, 83, 86, 88; metaphors, 79–80
life writing, 58, 60
Likud party, 5

literature, European *see* literature European; Hasidic, 64; Israeli *see* literature, Israeli; and television, 26–7; Yiddish, 64
literature, European, Modernism/ Existentialism, 3–4
literature, Israeli, early Modern, 12; ideology, 3; 'New Wave', 3; and Western literature, 4
Lover, The (A.B. Yehoshua), 80

Man Without Qualities (R. Musil), 50
Marquez, Garcia, 46
Marxism, 25
Megged, Matti, 59
memoirs, 58
memory, 91; and life writing, 60
metaphors, 79–80, 90
Michael, Sami, 3, 63; Arabic, writing in, 74–5; Iraq, escape from, 69, 70; Israel, arrival in, 69; on Jewish identity, 73, 74; Water Authority, work for, 75; *Water Touching Water*, 67–77; writing themes, 69
Michaels, Anne, 62
Mikdamot (S. Yizhar), 59
Miller, Dr, 87
Mintz, Alan, 58
Miron, Dan, 21
Mishani, Dror, 68
Mitchell, W.J.T., 25, 27, 28
Modernism, 3–4
Moked, Gabriel, 37, 47
Mozart Was Not a Jew (G. Avigur-Rotem), 91
Musil, Robert, 50
My First Sony (B. Barabash), 17

nation-state, rise of, 1
'National Thoughts' (Y. Amichai), 14
nationalism, European, 31; Jewish, role of Hebrew, 2; and language, 31; political task of, 1–2
neo-Judaism, 6
New Jew, 22, 30, 67–8; model of, 73; myth of, 6
'New Life' club (Jerusalem), 65
'New Wave' literature, 3
Nora, Pierre, 60
novel, and ideology, 30

One Hundred Years of Solitude (G. Marquez), 46
Orientalism (E. Said), 86
Oz, Amos, 59
Oz, Avraham, 37

Passover, 100
Philsoph, Eli, 76
Post Mortem (Y. Kaniuk), 43, 59
Post-Modernism, 17, 81, 87
Pure Element of Time (H. Be'er), 59
Purim, 100

Ramallah, *Dybbuk*, performance in, 82; opening of Khalil es-Sakakini Cultural Center, 81
Rapaport, Solomon Zeynwil, 82
representation, and ideology, 28; Marxist approach to, 25
Reuveni, Yotam, 87
Revivalist writers, 12–13
Rivlin, Yohanan, 80, 86–7
Rosendorf Quartet (N. Shaham), 27
Rothschild, Baron de, 39
Rubinstein, Amnon, 91
Russian Revolution, and Jewish life, 59

Sabra generation (1948), 4, 6
Sadan, D., 64
Scholem, Gershom, 21, 33, 64
Sealed Scrolls (N. Shaham), 59
self, discovery of, 4
Sephardim, 3, 67
Series (N. Shaham), 2–3, 4, 22–35; characterisation/plot, 23–5, 26; on Jew, definition, 31; and media, 22, 29; as microcosm of Jewish people, 27; truth telling, 29; words/pictures compared, 27, *see also* Shaham, Nathan
Sfarim, Mendele Mocher, 13
Shaham, Nathan, 2–3, 4; on abnormality of Jewish life, 25; on aesthetic issues, 28; filmmaking, involvement in, 26; on ideology and art, 29–31; on media, 26, 29; *Rosendorf Quartet*, 27; *Sefer Hatum*, 59; *Series* publication, 22–35; on Zionism, 33
Shai, Eli, 20
Shaked, Gershon, 65, 90, 94
Shamir, Moshe, 51, 64
Shoah (C. Landsmann), 101
shtetl, 64
'Sister Arts', 27
Socialism, 15
solidarity, 74
Somech, Sasson, 68, 69, 73, 75
Srayah, Sh., 37
State of Israel, foundation, 3, 67, 102
Story of a Life (Aharon Appelfeld), 3, 57–66; context, 59–60, *see also* Appelfeld, Aharon
stream of consciousness novel, *Last Jew* as, 47
Sukkot (Feast of Tabernacles), 99
syntax, 13

Talush (young intellectual), 14
Tammuz, Benjamin, 2, 15–17
Tchernichovsky, S., 13, 98
Tedeschi, Hannah, 80, 83, 86
television productions, as art form, 26–7
testimony, 49
Tlushim ('uprooted' young Jews), 58–59
'Troops of the Defenders of the Hebrew Language' (B. Tammuz), 15–17
Tsalhavim (S. Yizhar), 59
Tzenik, K., 46

Index

Ut Pictura Poesis, 27, 28

Vayomer vayelech, biblical text of, 83
visual image, 26

Wallach, Yona, 19–20
War of Independence (1948), 38, 41–2, 45, 46, 47; and Holocaust, 52
Water Touching Water (Sami Michael), 3, 67–77; characterisation/plot, 69–74; Creation, story of, 75, *see also* Michael, Sami
wedding, Jewish, 84–5
Weitzman, Ezer, 11
West Bank, 86
Whither (M.Z. Feierberg), 14, 58
words, and imagery, 27

Yehoshua, A.B., 3, 5, 67, 68, 78–89, 90; on civilizations, 78–9; on *Dybbuk*, 80–1, 82, 83, 86, 88; on identity, 82–3; on neo-Judaism, 6
Yeuveni, Yotam, 85
Yiddish, 13, 100
Yizhar, S., 4–5, 59, 64
Yom Kippur, 100

Zach, Natan, 59, 75
Zaydoun, Nazim Ibn, 81
Zionism, 1; Brenner on, 15; early, 22, 31; and Holocaust, 71; ideology, 3, 5, 14, 16; Shaham on, 33
Zionist dream, 1, 3, 93; revisionist view, 17
Zionist movement, 68
Zorba the Greek (Nikos Kazantzakis), 99

Also published by Vallentine Mitchell

New Women's Writing from Israel
Risa Domb (ed.)

Choice Outstanding Academic Book, 1996

£40.00 / £19.50, 1996, 240 pages
ISBN 0 85303 307 2 and 0 85303 308 0

Home Thoughts from Abroad
Distant Visions of Israel
in Contemporary Hebrew Fiction
Risa Domb

This is the first critique of modern Hebrew literature to examine the vital concept of place.

£35.00 / £18.50, 1995, 128 pages
ISBN 0 85303 303 X and 0 85303 304 8

The Arab in Hebrew Prose 1911–1948
Risa Domb

£29.50, 1982, 180 pages
ISBN 0 85303 203 3

Also published by Vallentine Mitchell

Contemporary Israeli Women's Writing
Risa Domb

During the nineteenth and early twentieth century, women could not participate in the development of Modern Hebrew literature. As pointed out in the Introduction to Volume I, they could give vent to their poetic talents either in Yiddish, their spoken language, or in Russian, but not in Hebrew. In the 1920s Hebrew prose was more open to autobiographical and confessional writing, and women were able to contribute to this genre, as they could incorporate the full range of their experience. It was only with the next generation of writers, the generation of 'The New Wave' writers of the 1960s and 1970s, that women's prose writing found its niche. The change in the mainstream Israeli experience meant greater openness in literature, and a pluralism of voices emerged, incorporating those of women writers. As a result, they could, at last, as was shown in Volume I, abandon their traditional place in Hebrew literature and assume their rightful role in its development. Since the 1980s a great deal has changed. Israeli Women's writing became more consciously feminist, asserting feminist ideology and representing it in their work. Furthermore, we hear for the first time the voices of women who express their experience of religious life. Either from within Jewish orthodoxy, or more often having left this world, they offer us a glimpse into this hitherto unknown literary terrain. Interestingly, many still use the marvelous genre of the short story. Volume II will reflect these dramatic changes.

2007

Also published by Vallentine Mitchell

Ruth Borchardt, an 'Enemy Alien' in Holloway Prison
'The strangest times of our lives'

Ruth Borchardt's *We Are Strangers Here*, reproduced here with an introduction by Charmian Brinson, was written but not completed in 1943, and only came to light after the author's recent death. The novel vividly describes the plight of a young German refugee, Anna Silver, as an 'enemy alien' in Britain on the outbreak of war, and her subsequent detention in Holloway Prison, a situation made more complex by her young child.

The novel finishes as Anna Silver arrives at the Internment Camp on the Isle of Man; the second part of the novel, dealing with events on the Isle of Man, was planned but appears never to have been written. This book highlights the plight of German anti-Nazis and Jews in British exile and has a distinct air of tragicomedy about it.

Little has been written on the internment of women during the Second World War, and this book will appeal to readers interested in modern history, social history and women's studies.

2007
150 pages

Also published by Vallentine Mitchell

Israel on Israel
John Laughland and Michel Korinman (eds.)

Nowhere is the debate about Israel and its future stronger than in Israel itself. Politicians, academics and journalists from Israel and the wider world join forces in this volume to discuss the various existential questions which face their state. What, if anything, has changed in Palestinian politics since the death of Yasir Arafat? What are the differences between European and American approaches to the Israeli question? Why does the Palestinian cause continue to excite so much support in the West? Is the idea of a two-state solution still viable? What is the reality of Zionism and why is it so often demonised? What is the role of historians in understanding the history of the state of Israel and influencing the policies of today? What is the role of Arab citizens in Israel? How was the construction of the security barrier decided, and how was the precise route traced? What has been the effect has the immigration of Russian and Ethiopian Jews to Israel? What is the role of religion in Israeli politics?

£49.50 / £18.50, 2006, 360 pages
ISBN 0 85303 657 8 and 0 85303 658 6

Also published by Vallentine Mitchell

Deadly Carousel
A Singer's Story of the Second World War
Monica Porter

In March 1944 eleven divisions of German troops marched into Hungary. Thousands of Jews were rounded up and deported to death camps. Desperately, they sought foreign diplomatic relations, false identity papers and hiding places.

Vali Rácz was a successful singer and film actress, the darling of the Hungarian public. Since she was young, beautiful and safely Aryan, the Nazis represented no particular threat to her, but she was horrified by the persecution of the Jews, many of whom were friends and mentors. Risking her own life, she turned her villa in Buda into a secret refuge.

Monica Porter traces both the life of her remarkable and courageous mother and a fascinating period in Hungarian history.

In September 1991 the Jewish people's highest expression of gratitude was conferred upon Vali Rácz in Jerusalem: the title of 'Righteous among the Nations'.

£17.50, 2006, 200 pages
ISBN 0 85303 700 0

Also published by Vallentine Mitchell

ADAM
An Anthology of Miron Grindea's *ADAM* Editorials
Rachel Lasserson

ADAM International Review was the longest-running literary magazine to exist under one editor. It started life in Romania as a Jewish magazine, but relocated to Britain, where its editor, Miron Grindea, sought refuge from Nazi-occupied Europe. It first appeared in 1941 and continued to challenge and entertain its readers until Grindea's death in 1995 brought its lively story to an end. He was working on number 500 when he died.

The life of *ADAM* reflects the main currents in literary and artistic life through five decades, and the magazine counts among its contributors Picasso, Bertolt Brecht, Graham Greene, Jean Cocteau, Ungaretti, André Gide, François Mauriac, Walt Whitman, W. H. Auden, Igor Stravinsky and Benjamin Britten.

ADAM introduced the British reader to writing from all around the world – Chile, India, Sweden, Senegal, Ecuador – long before the translation industry had made global literature standard fare. However, French culture was Grindea's greatest passion and he dedicated *ADAM* to the task of cultural bridge-building between Britain and France. He believed that the artist and the intellectual had a responsibility to further the task of an active humanism.

Volume 1
£45.00 / £19.95, 2006, 260 pages
ISBN 0 85303 623 3 and 0 85303 624 1
Volume 2
£45.00 / £19.95, 2006, 200 pages
ISBN 0 85303 666 7 and 0 85303 667 5

Also published by Vallentine Mitchell

German Writers in French Exile, 1933–1940
Martin Mauthner

This book is an account of what happened to some of the best German writers and journalists after they fled the Nazi terror to find shelter in France. It is a tragic intellectual drama that unfolds over seven years, and features writers such as Thomas Mann, Lion Feuchtwanger, Stefan Zweig and Joseph Roth, as well as H. G. Wells, André Malraux, Aldous Huxley and André Gide. It recounts how persecuted writers settled in a colony in the south of France, how they tried to counter-attack, aided by British and French writers, how they quarrelled among themselves and how they sought to alert the West to Nazi plans for military conquest and warn the German people that Hitler was plunging the nation into ruin.

£45.00 / £19.50, 2006, 256 pages
ISBN 0 85303 540 7 and 0 85303 541 5

Also published by Vallentine Mitchell

Opportunities That Pass
An Historical Miscellany
Cecil Roth

Cecil Roth was the first Anglo-Jewish historian to become a household name. In addition to his numerous books, Roth wrote many articles for a wide range of journals in Britain and overseas, notably in America, on Jewish life and history. This volume comprises a substantial collection of them, selected for their special and continuing Jewish appeal and human interest, none of which have appeared in book form before.

£37.50 / £17.95, 2005, 208 pages
ISBN 0 85303 575 X and 0 85303 576 8

Also published by Vallentine Mitchell

Commentary Magazine
A Journal of Significant Thought and Opinion
Nathan Abrams

Launched in 1945, *Commentary* magazine became one of America's most celebrated periodicals. Under the editorship of Elliot E. Cohen, it developed into the premier post-war journal of Jewish affairs, attracting a readership far wider than is Jewish community origin. This book is the first detailed and critical study of *Commentary* magazine during its formative years. Abrams traces the development of the key issues that have occupied its first fifty years: the construction of a new American Jewish identity, Judaism, the Holocaust, the State of Israel, and the Cold War. This account of the most influential journal of Jewish thought, opinion, and culture in America will complete the picture of post-war American Jewish and general intellectual life. It is based on a wide range of sources including archival and other material never before published in the context of *Commentary* magazine.

£45.00 / £19.95, 2005, 244 pages
ISBN 0 85303 663 2 and 0 85303 664 0

Also published by Vallentine Mitchell

Anglo-Jewish Poetry from Isaac Rosenberg to Elaine Feinstein
Peter Lawson

This is the first book-length study to survey the phenomenon of twentieth-century Anglo-Jewish poetry. It proceeds by reading established Anglo-Jewish poets against the grain of conventional thinking about English verse. For example, rather than understanding Isaac Rosenberg and Siegfried Sassoon as simply First World War poets, it approaches them as minority Anglo-Jewish poets as well. A similar challenge to the notion of undifferentiated English literature is made with respect to four other major writers: John Rodker, Jon Silkin, Elaine Feinstein and Karen Gershon. All these poets share a peripheral relationship with English and Jewish culture, together with a common attachment to the diasporic narrative of exile and deferred return to a textually imagined homeland.

£45.00 / £19.50, 2005, 228 pages
ISBN 0 85303 616 0 and 0 85303 617 9

Also published by Vallentine Mitchell

Composers of Classical Music of Jewish Descent
Lewis Stevens

This important book attempts to analyse the reasons for the predominance in classical music of composers of Jewish descent while highlighting their role within the production of works of significance, particularly over the last two hundred years. Written in two parts, the larger second section provides an invaluable compilation of biographical sketches for over 250 composers.

£45.00 / £19.95, 2005, 256 pages
ISBN 0 85303 482 6 and 0 85303 613 6

Also published by Vallentine Mitchell

Gender and Israeli Society
New Studies from Israel
Hanneh Naveh

This is the first of two interconnected volumes engaging with the concept of 'women's time' and recounts stories and histories of women, along with other marginalized groups, categories and classes, and places them back into history.

£45.00 / £17.95, 2004, 198 pages
ISBN 0 85303 504 0 and 0 85303 503 2

Israeli Family and Community
Women's Time
Hanneh Naveh

This book uses a new concept of 'Time' to examine women's role in the family in Israel. It brings a feminist gaze to a wide variety of fascinating issues facing contemporary Israeli society, first by examining the private, natural sphere of women's experience, and then by addressing the interaction between the private and the national spheres as reflected in the media and in religious and military discourse.

£45.00 / £17.95, 2004, 198 pages
ISBN 0 85303 506 7 and 0 85303 505 9

Also published by Vallentine Mitchell

Myths in Israeli Culture
Captives of a Dream
Nurith Gertz

An analysis of texts, written before and after the establishment of the State of Israel, selected from the spheres of literature, journalism, politics, cinema and television, which casts light on the modern history of Israel.

£45.00 / £18.95, 2000, 192 pages
ISBN 0 85303 386 2 and 0 85303 383 8

Also published by Vallentine Mitchell

Holocaust Literature
Schulz, Levi, Spiegelman and the Memory of the Offence
Gillian Banner

This book provides an evaluation of the dynamics of memory in relation to representations of the Holocaust. It examines the compulsion to remember, the dilemmas of representation, and the relationship between memory, knowledge and belief in the works of Bruno Schulz, Primo Levi and Art Spiegelman.

£45.00 / £17.95, 2000, 184 pages
ISBN 0 85303 364 1 and 0 85303 371 4